Doing the Business

Boost Your Company's Fortunes

David Hall

Dedication
This book is dedicated to my four children Simon, Darren, Natalie and Penny, who help me not to take myself too seriously.

First published in Great Britain in 2002 by
Virgin Books Ltd
Thames Wharf Studios
Rainville Road
London
W6 9HA

ISBN 0 7535 0680 7

Series Consultant: Professor David Storey
Joint Series Editors: Robert Craven, Grier Palmer

Series design by Janice Mather at Ben Cracknell Studios
Typeset by Phoenix Photosetting, Chatham, Kent
Printed and bound in Great Britain by Mackays of Chatham

Contents

Acknowledgements

My sincere thanks to:
The entrepreneurs who have shared their wisdom for the benefit of others; Kirstie Addis and Humphrey Price at Virgin Books for commissioning this book; Angela Mason, my personal assistant, who produced the manuscript.

The stories in this book are used to illustrate how the toolkits have been used in practice. In some cases the entrepreneurs requested that their identities be not revealed in their stories for commercial reasons.

Many thanks to all those entrepreneurs who allowed us to use their stories for the benefit of others.

Disclaimer

Foreword
by Sir Richard Branson

It feels a bit odd to be writing a foreword to a business book. Perhaps it's because I haven't always done business by the book myself. Sometimes I've regretted that, and sometimes I've been glad that I followed my instincts instead of doing what conventional advisers might have recommended.

One thing I've learned is that there's no right way to do things in life. There is no 'magic bullet' for success in business. What works for Virgin Atlantic might not be right for British Airways; what suits your business could be completely wrong for someone else's. But any advice that can help you beat the odds and succeed in business has got to be a good thing. Listening to lots of people's ideas before taking a decision has always been something I have strongly believed in.

Every book in this series has been written by an expert in his or her field, and they've come up with lots of interesting and thought-provoking ideas. But the most important thing is to do what you personally feel is right.

Business should be fun. Enjoy what you do, and success comes within reach.

Good luck!

Preface

The central theme of this book, and perhaps the Virgin series as a whole, is that those running their own businesses learn most effectively from the experience of others who have been, or who are in the same position themselves. As David Hall says, 'this is a book for businesspeople by businesspeople'.

Of course not everyone who runs a business can distil the wisdom that they have accumulated and place it in an 'easy learning' context. David Hall's approach to distillation is to produce a set of 33 practical toolkits that are ways of getting things done in your own business. Almost half of these deal with aspects internal to the business and the remainder focus upon external relationships.

So what does a toolkit do? Essentially it divides a simple, step-by-step procedure for addressing an issue in the business in a way that leads to a clear improvement. Frequently the step-by-step approach is then linked to an example of a real business that has actually used the toolkit to generate improvement. Since there are 33 toolkits, David Hall encourages you to pick'n'mix as you choose. So some readers might plump for a relatively tight toolkit: 'fixing system slippage', or 'fighting the flab' – which is really another way of saying 'cost cutting'; others, however, might choose the more generic toolkits such as 'being interpersonally skilled' or 'providing leadership'.

Of course the ones you choose to read first, or which ring true most powerfully, say as much about you as they do about your business. For example, I kept coming back to, and feeling that David Hall had scored rather too many bull's-eyes on, toolkit six. This is about 'tools for prioritising and focusing'. Here the author makes the easy point that we should 'work smarter and not harder'; of course doing it is something else. David Hall challenges you to identify in your strategy or plan objectives such as cost reduction, improving market share, building brands, delighting customers etc. What he then asks you to do is to review your diary during the last month and ask whether you have been spending your time in accordance with these priorities. There may be readers who satisfactorily pass this test, but I suspect that many, like me, will sheepishly have to admit that any resemblance between objectives and time allocation is purely coincidental!

There is no better illustration of David Hall's strategy of challenging you to address important issues and then to helping you seek to address the problems.

Professor David Storey
Director, Centre for Small and Medium Sized Enterprises
Warwick Business School, University of Warwick

Introduction

Are you ready to boost your business's fortunes?

The toolkits in *Doing the Business* have been developed and used by a whole range of businesses, many of which make personal appearances as the stars of this book.

> ■ 'The toolkits helped us to boost our profits way beyond our expectations.' – Simon Keats, MD, North Staffs Caravans.
>
> ■ 'We used David's toolkits to redo our strategy, remove the blockages to our progress and get control of our business. They transformed our performance.' – Dave Osmond, sales and marketing director, CompuAdd Computer Group.
>
> ■ 'The toolkits gave our managers lots of new ideas to help them to revitalise our business.' – Neil Whitley, vice-president, Oil and Gas Synetix ICI.

So, whether you want to grow, revitalise or reinvent your business, *Doing the Business* could help you, too.

A key theme in this book is that businesspeople prefer to get their ideas on how to develop their business from experienced businesspeople who have already tackled the problems and opportunities they currently face.

Doing the Business puts you in touch with successful businesspeople who have been there and done it. Let's take an example: say you want to find some new ideas to increase your sales. What options do you normally have?

- trial and error
- read a theoretical textbook
- hire a consultant
- go on a course

How attractive do these options sound? In reality they often fail to help you to solve your problems. But what if you could tap into the wisdom of a successful businessperson to help you to boost your sales?

Here's the best bit. *Doing the Business* goes further than that. I have consolidated the wisdom from dozens of successful businesspeople into a set of practical toolkits to help you to boost your business.

I asked businesspeople what they wanted and they told me the book should be fad-free and practical, but most of all it should be based on the wisdom of successful businesspeople.

So here it is. A book for businesspeople by businesspeople.

The book's key principles

Whatever you do should be based on the needs of your business right now and not the latest management fad. Eighty per cent of fads are abandoned within twelve months. This book is a 'fad-free zone'.

There is no magic formula for success. This apparently does not stop so-called 'management gurus' promising divine redemption if only you buy their latest potions that cure all ills. The toolkits provide a process to help you develop your business, but these are not a magic formula.

The wisdom to make your business work resides within, not with external 'experts'. It's always amazed me that businesses allow pinstriped consultants who have no experience of their business to tell them what to do. A key principle in this book is to use your team to help you develop your business – the wisdom is within and it's much more cost-effective.

Managers value processes (toolkits) to help them to find and use the internal wisdom on behalf of the business. They also value learning from successful peers. It has proved very helpful to provide managers with toolkits to help them to mine this internal wisdom. The toolkits are based on the wisdom of successful businesspeople.

Balancing key stakeholders' needs provides the best chance of long-term success. There are now numerous studies that show that success in the long run comes to those businesses that seek to balance the interests of customers, employees and shareholders. Whenever one of these stakeholders gets too much or too little the business overall normally suffers.

Success is possible for everyone. Creating a successful business takes a lot of hard work and some luck, but it is within the grasp of everyone.

Getting the most out of doing the business

Here are some tips to help you to get the most out of *Doing the Business*.

Working on the business

The people in this book all work *on* as well as *in* their businesses. Working in the business means attending to the day-to-day operational problems. However, if you don't make a conscious effort to work *on* your business, it can never really significantly improve. The toolkits are designed to help you to stand back, take a fresh look and work *on* your business in order to boost its fortunes.

Here are some of the reasons some people give for not working *on* their business.

'We don't have time; we're too busy.'
Time is usually a lame excuse. If a major issue turns up you make time to fix it. Lack of time really means, 'It's not a priority for us' or 'We don't understand the benefits' or even 'That sounds like too much trouble.'

Working *on* the business is about working smarter, not harder. It will boost the fortunes of your business just as it has for many other businesses in this book.

'We don't have the resources to work on the business.'
One of the key findings from my work is that a major reason that businesses are unable to change or innovate is that they have a blind spot about making the resources available. That's why it is helpful to consider the costs and benefits of working on your business. One MD found that using one toolkit had the potential of doubling their profits; he quickly changed his mind about making the resources available!

'We don't know how to work on the business, so we keep our heads down even though at times I think we are busy fools.'
That's why I developed these toolkits. I found that businesses do need processes that help them to improve their business fortunes.

Right, you have no excuses for not working *on* your business, so let's get on with it.

New perspectives, new opportunities

The toolkits help you to create some new perspectives on your business. This means raising your consciousness level to enable you to spot opportunities to develop your business. Raising consciousness levels means seeing things from a new perspective.

For example:

- The first time you conduct a customer perception survey (Toolkit 16) can be very revealing. This lets you see your business as your customers do and usually provides some real shocks and new insights.
- Role-clarification feedback (Toolkit 12) can be very helpful to people because it raises their consciousness level about how people around them really do see them.
- Visiting a restaurant in the USA for the first time can raise consciousness levels about how fantastic customer service (Toolkit 18) can be when it's done really well.

These new insights can be a bit scary to start with but afterwards people often say, 'I wish I'd been aware of this earlier.'

New perspectives create opportunities to learn. Stepping outside your comfort zone to see things from a different perspective can create opportunities you never dreamed about, because they were outside your existing consciousness level.

Traditional business approaches such as SWOT (strengths, weaknesses, opportunities, threats) analysis, market research and business planning provide important perspectives on your business. The toolkits presented in *Doing the Business* – such as 'Fixing system slippage', 'Inspect, don't expect' and 'Let go to grow' – provide quite different perspectives and so create completely new entrepreneurial opportunities to boost your business. This was the primary aim in writing this book.

A doing-the-business mindset

Increasingly, businesspeople are recognising that getting into the right frame of mind is a critical part of the recipe for success. Sports people have worked at getting their mental attitude right for years.

Here is the *Doing the Business* mindset that seems really to help with the successful application of the toolkits.

A 'can do' attitude: Most successful entrepreneurs have faith and belief that they can solve problems, remove blocks and achieve success. They are in control of their destiny.

Being realistic: Be sensible about what can be achieved. Let's be neither naïvely optimistic ('This will change my world') nor deeply cynical ('We've seen this all before').

Operating in learning mode: 'We don't have the answers, but let's see if we can learn how to do this.' 'Let's be prepared to try different ways, take a few risks, and give it a go.'

Being action-orientated: Get on and do something rather than talk about it. Get momentum into your *Doing the Business* work.

Being the leader: Sometimes business teams seem to go through the motions and do not really engage in the process. Act as a role model and provide the leadership to encourage your people to take it seriously.

Provide the vision, passion and energy to inspire your people to really boost your business.

> TIP: Listen to how successful businesspeople talk about how they do business. See if you can spot these attitudes in them.

Introducing the toolkits

The wisdom of successful businesspeople is translated into step-by-step toolkits, to help you to achieve your goals. While providing guidance, the toolkits leave you in control; you should adapt them to your business needs. In order to bring the toolkits to life some of the stories that helped shape them are included.

In one sense the toolkits provide the thinking (head) while the stories provide the inspiration (heart).

The toolkits consist of various parts.

Stories
Businesspeople telling their stories to illustrate the use of the toolkit in practice. In most stories the businesspeople are named unless they sought anonymity for commercial reasons.

A step-by-step process
In most toolkits the steps are sequential, but in toolkits 4, 6, 23 and 26 the steps are not sequential.

Examples
Short examples are provided to illustrate key points.

Tips
Tips are provided by businesspeople – wisdom from their experience.

Troubleshooter
The potential problems and suggested remedies from the experiences of businesspeople using the toolkit.

Toolkits	
Title	**Purpose**
1: How to achieve your personal goals (p.11)	Achieve your hopes and aspirations.
2: Developing your business skills (p.16)	Ensure your business continues to improve by developing your business skills.
3: Developing your personal qualities (p.21)	Develop your creative and innovation skills.
4: Being interpersonally skilled (p.27)	Build strong relationships.
5: Providing leadership (p.34)	Produce results beyond expectations.
6: Tools for prioritising and focusing (p.39)	Work smarter, not harder.
7: Working on the business (p.43)	Significantly improve the performance of your business in all aspects.
8: Creating a vision for your business (p.50)	Provide focus and direction for everybody in your business.
9: Redoing your strategy in order to revitalise your business (p.55)	Focus on your business strengths (internally) and market opportunities (externally).

Title	Purpose
10: Managing stakeholders effectively (p.64)	Ensure positive support from your key stakeholders.
11: Picking the right people (p.69)	Avoid expensive mistakes and, even worse, mediocrity.
12: Clarify the key roles in your business (p.74)	Ensure your key resources are focused on the right priorities for your business.
13: How to achieve your business goals by really motivating your top team (p.80)	Ensure your top team is individually motivated.
14: Dealing with supervisory slippage (p.82)	Set and maintain high standards.
15: Let go to grow (p.86)	Delegate successfully in order to grow your business and yourself.
16: Conducting a customer perception survey (p.91)	Review your business through your customers' eyes.
17: Removing the obstacles your customers face buying from you (p.100)	Make it easy for customers to do business with you.
18: Getting customer service right (p.105)	Create sustainable competitive advantage.
19: Build your business by delighting customers (p.112)	Increase customer loyalty, get new customers from referrals and reduce price sensitivity.
20: Build your business by networking (p.121)	Create and maintain relationships with people who can help you to build your business.
21: Problem seeking, problem solving, to create opportunities (p.127)	Get really close to your customers.
22: Increasing sales using the turnover drivers (p.131)	Use the six turnover drivers to really boost sales.
23: 'Intrepreneurship': innovate and reinvent your business (p.138)	Bring Silicon valley into your business.
24: Developing a superior product or service (p.145)	Gain a larger share of your customers' business.
25: Using the EntreNet to really boost your business (p.152)	Share the wisdom within your business in order to boost its performance.
26: Making work fun and enjoyable (p.158)	Increase motivation, commitment and creativity.

What's your problem?

The toolkits have been used in a number of ways to solve business problems. There is no one right way of using them. Here are some examples of ways in which businesspeople have used them, to get your juices flowing and help you to make a start on boosting your business.

People have used ideas or bits from individual toolkits. For example, the ground rules in toolkit 28, 'Fixing system slippage', can be used to set up any 'group-think' activity. Some have used a full toolkit from start to finish. For instance, Simon Keats, MD of North Staffs Caravans, followed 'Fixing system slippage' to the letter: 'The toolkit produced results way beyond our expectations,' he says.

Combinations of toolkits can be used sequentially to tackle a complex problem. Let us look at some examples.

Example A

A regional newspaper group wanted to get a lot closer to their customers, so they used the Customerising group of toolkits.

The use of Toolkit 16, 'Conducting a customer perception survey', identified the need for Toolkit 17, 'Removing the obstacles to your customers buying from you'. They then decided to review their whole customer service process, so they used Toolkit 18, 'Getting customer service right'.

Finally they wanted to increase customer loyalty, so they

used Toolkit 19, 'Building your business to delight your customers'.

Example B

CompuAdd used a different combination of toolkits to meet their needs. First, they used Toolkit 9, 'Redoing your strategy in order to revitalise your business'. Once the strategy was sorted, they decided that they needed to control the new strategy, so they used Toolkit 30, 'Control your recipe for success'.

This led to the recognition that they needed to improve in some key areas, so they used Toolkit 7, 'Working on the business'.

'The whole process got us back on track and boosted our profits,' says Martin Vincent, their CEO.

Example C

Synetix, a business within ICI, were looking to develop their business. They appointed six internal 'intrepreneurs' (these are people who practise the values of entrepreneurs within their own businesses) to lead the change process and made the whole 33 toolkits available to their team to support them in the process of growing and developing the business.

So you can see that it is possible and highly desirable to use any combination of the toolkits that you feel may help you solve your problems or take up any new opportunities.

If you have a burning issue, then start there. My friend Gerard Egan, a management consultant, told me, 'Start where the pain is and build from there.' That's not a bad tip.

A logical sequence

I am reluctant to be too prescriptive in telling you which toolkits to select. It clearly depends on your own unique situation. However, there is a logic to the sequence of the toolkits, which may help you to decide where to start.

Getting you sorted out personally at the start seemed a good beginning, so the first group, 'Building your own capability' (Toolkits 1–6), are all about you. I think you are important and I hope you do, too. So, if you do not have a burning issue, why not start with you? You are a critical role model and major influence.

'Working on the business' (Toolkit 7) is a generic one that can be used in combination with many of the others. That's why it's next in the sequence.

Getting strategy straight is always a first for me (Toolkits 8–10). If you get that straight, a lot of other things fall into place and priorities become obvious.

Teams come before customers. Sir Richard Branson always opens his mail from his team first. Why? He believes (rightly, in my view) that a turned-on team is essential to delivering good service. If you give good service then customers will pay you and everybody is happy! Not a bad logic. So see 'Developing your team' (Toolkits 11–15).

Success happens in the marketplace, so 'Customerising: getting much closer to your customers' (16–19) come next. Without customers all you have are costs, so looking after them is critical.

Selling more to existing customers and creating new customers is the next group of toolkits: 'Creating sales' (20–22).

Good marketing cannot make up for a poor product in the long run, so great businesses create great products and services. 'Developing new products and services' (23–24) comes next.

On the inside

That's the external stuff done. Time now to look inside your business.

Sorting out strategy gives you the *what*; building your culture provides the *how*: how we do things around here. Toolkits 25–27 help you build your preferred culture rather than get a weak culture by default.

The 'Become more efficient and effective' group (Toolkits 28–29) will create funds to reinvest in your business, improve your service levels and boost your efficiency and effectiveness.

Many businesses are haemorrhaging costs and profits. The easiest way to make money is to stop losing it. See 'Cut costs, boost profits' (Toolkits 30–1).

Finally, 'Controlling your business' (Toolkits 32–3) enables you to sleep easy in your bed, knowing that your business is under control.

You may well disagree with the batting order that I have selected – and that's fine. Remember our key principle: 'no magic formula'. You start where it feels right for you, and that will probably be the right place. And the very best of luck with using *Doing the Business* in *your* business.

CHAPTER ONE

Building Your Own Capability

Toolkits 1–6

Toolkit 1: How to achieve your personal goals
Toolkit 2: Developing your business skills
Toolkit 3: Developing your personal qualities
Toolkit 4: Being interpersonally skilled
Toolkit 5: Providing leadership
Toolkit 6: Tools for prioritising and focusing

Toolkit 1 – How to achieve your personal goals

- Achieve your hopes and aspirations.
- Learn from high performing people.
- Get real focus and direction in your life.

This is a very personal toolkit – it's about you and your future. It's the first toolkit because it helps you create your personal vision and therefore the context for everything else you do in your business. Achieving personal goals is usually part of most people's dreams. However, in practice we can also create our own barriers to our success. The good news is that we can also choose to remove the same barriers and that is what this toolkit is about. So let's get started.

Story – A Young Entrepreneur

'Get a trade' was the well-meaning advice from a mother to her son in the summer of 1964. So together with his mates he became an apprentice builder earning £2.50 per week. He hated every minute of it because he didn't seem to have the necessary skills to build things: walls fell down, pipes leaked, his boss got angry ...

One day another well-meaning person, the company training manager, sent the young man for a vocational guidance assessment, during which he was told that he had the personality and skills to become a 'lawyer, a journalist or a management consultant' – jobs that require the ability to persuade people orally or in writing.

This seemed a million miles away to a 23-year-old with no qualifications, a mortgage and two children. 'You should get a degree' was a further wake-up call.

The young man began to dream dreams about becoming a consultant, building a business, writing books and maybe even starring in a TV series.

The dream became clearer, choices were made and a clear focus emerged. He would become a management consultant, build a business and become famous.

One O level by correspondence, then five O levels at night school, followed by a diploma in management studies and a master's degree in management led to the assertion by his wife that he had become 'overdeveloped from the neck upwards'.

A second apprenticeship was served in evenings and at weekends. 'My day job and the night job,' he called them. The night job involved learning to become a consultant by doing market research and cost studies, which trainee consultants have to do to earn their spurs.

In 1982 he quit his full-time job in business development with Steetley PLC and set up as a management consultant from his dining table at home.

The dream began to turn into reality: 'My vision enabled me to keep going, putting in the hours believing that one day I would get there.'

He built a £5 million business employing 120 people from fourteen offices in the UK and sold it as a management buyout in 1996. In 1992 the young entrepreneur wrote an award-winning TV business series for the BBC, *Winning*.

'I achieved my dream by staying focused and believing that I could be successful and taking the breaks when they came along. The drive came from being poor and not wanting to be poor again and somebody helping me to raise my aspirations in order to become the best that I could be.'

The young entrepreneur is an older entrepreneur now – and still dreaming …

Ringing the changes

Achieving our goals often means changing the way we do things, but change can be very difficult and can be traumatic for people depending upon how they perceive it.

Most change is perceived as discretionary – 'I have a choice' – so we often decide not to change. Nondiscretionary change on the other hand normally does lead to change and therefore success.

Nondiscretionary change is normally driven by pain or discomfort with the present situation, so you want to change things in order to relieve the discomfort. Your ability to change depends on this time-tested formula: $C = P \times V \times A$, where C (change) is driven by: P, your level of pain ('We just failed to land a really big critical order we desperately needed …'); V, vision or objectives ('To be the market leader in our sector …'); and A, action ('I've joined a health club to get fit in body and mind').

Here is how to apply this change formula in order to remove the barriers to the achievement of your vision.

Step 1: Create the pain
Thinking about your life generally, ask yourself these two very tough questions:

1. In my life right now why am I doing what I am doing?
Be really honest with yourself, try to stop faking it. We get only one life and this is it. This is not a dress rehearsal. Very often the answer eventually is: 'I'm not sure …'

This is a good answer because, as a wise mentor of mine says, 'At the moment of uncertainty we often get our biggest insights and breakthroughs.'

2. Who am I doing this for?
Another tough question. Many people go through their lives trying to please everybody but themselves and end up miserable as a result. So

stop faking it. Who are you really doing it for? Go on, try being brutally honest.

> TIP: This is important because it may be one of the barriers to your personal success and happiness.

Hopefully, answering these questions will have helped you to identify what you don't want and may even have been painful. Facing an unpleasant truth can be difficult. That's the bad news. But you will now be ready to take Step 2 – and ask yourself what you want. This could be the start of the new you, and that's the good news.

> TIP: This is a personal process, not one to share with lots of people, regardless of how close they may be to you. This is about you.

Step 2: Ask yourself: What do I really want?

Write your answers down. Go for quantity at this stage and write down as many as possible. Keep a notebook and write down your thoughts as they come to you. This maybe over a period of time. Some examples: I want to be rich, travel extensively, see more of my kids, be famous, have a TV series, be healthy, own a £100 million business, retire at fifty.

Asking the following questions can help with your goal-generation process:

- What am I really good at?
- What would I like to get really good at?
- What part of my life/job do I really enjoy?
- When time flies what have I usually been doing?
- What footprint do I want to leave in the sand when I am gone?
- What would I like to see on my gravestone?
- What would I like to be remembered for?

Answer these questions seriously. Remember: it's you you're sorting out and you are important. After all, you're worth it.

Step 3: Prioritise your list to identify your real goals

There are many ways of prioritising: you can rate each of your thoughts in Step 2 out of 100 (1 = low, 100 = perfect), or you can rate the ideas against each other until you get down to one or two real goals, such as: 'I want to be rich' versus 'I want to be healthy'. I decided I wanted to be healthy so I eliminated being rich.

Carry on comparing and eliminating until you end up with one or two goals. This again is a tough task – eliminating goals. One of the biggest blockages to success, however, is having too many priorities – 'I have twenty goals'. This inevitably dissipates energy, so you are in grave danger of doing twenty things to a poor or average standard.

The secret of high-performance people is one word: focus. Great sports stars, film stars, politicians and businesspeople usually have a clear vision, which helps them to:

- Focus their energies upon it.
- Make choices – 'I will do that if it helps me move towards my goals'.
- Decide how to spend their time.
- Gather all sorts of information in order to achieve their goal – obsessive commitment: it brings a new perspective to what they notice and think about.

Here are some example goals from friends who have completed this exercise:

- 'To be as good as I can possibly be at what I do.'
- 'To love and cherish my children.'
- 'To contribute to a stable, progressive and modern society.'
- 'To achieve a successful balance between work, family and interests.'
- 'To be happy and enjoy myself.'

Write your goal(s) here (maximum two, preferably one): My goal is

....

....

Step 4: Take action

Once you have established your goals, most planning processes would now say make a detailed plan. But detailed plans don't fire the imagination: actions do. If a journey of a thousand miles starts with one step then what is the first step (action) you need to take right now in order to move you closer to your goal?

After you take the first step the second, third and fourth will become obvious – you don't need to write them down, but you will need to think them through. However, if you like making detailed plans then do so, but don't confuse this with action taking.

> TIP: Write down on a card your goal and the actions you want to take. Read the card frequently to put your vision into your subconscious mind so it can help you achieve your goals. For example, goal: 'make work fun'; first action: eliminate some of the tasks I hate by delegating them to more competent people than me; goal: 'spend time with children'; first action: put birthdays and the important family dates in my diary, underline them in red and make them non-negotiable.

Step 5: Analyse your personal strengths and turn them into motivators

Ask yourself: 'What am I really, really good at?' Then use this to motivate you to achieve your goal. For example, the management consultant Gerard Egan wants to 'leave an imprint in the sand' with his original work on counselling and management models. One strength is that he is a brilliant and inspiring conference speaker. He therefore uses conference platforms around the world to get his message across about his models. Consequently his books have now been translated in fourteen different languages.

What are your strengths and how can you use them to help you achieve your goals?

Summary

Do you now feel you have a clear focus? If you have then the rest of the toolkits will help you to achieve your aspirations.

Toolkit 2 – Developing your business skills

> ■ Ensure your business continues to improve by developing your business skills.
> ■ Develop your confidence and competence as a Top Manager.
> ■ Continue to learn, grow and enjoy your work.

The key principle here is both business and management development. 'Develop the managers and the business develops' is a truism found in every enterprise. If your business is stagnating, tired and no fun any more this may reflect where you are right now.

When did you last invest in *you*? Have you stopped learning – other than day-to-day problem solving? When did you last get a personal MOT? It may be time to get going again and to invest in developing yourself and your business. Here are three time-tested ways to do it. Pick the one that suits you.

1. Delivering your strategy
2. Developing business competencies
3. Hiring a personal coach

1. Delivering your strategy

Considering your business strategy (mission, vision, values, products and markets). What does your strategy demand that you personally need to do well or differently right now in order to ensure its successful implementation?

Example

> - develop a strong team
> - find new opportunities
> - create new customers
> - raise capital for investment
> - drive down costs etc.

List them here:

....

....

Consider completing Toolkit 12, 'Clarify the roles in your business' – this will help you to clarify your priorities. Which skills do you already possess and which do you need to develop? Ask your colleagues for an objective view. Summarise your business-skills development needs.

Example: A CEO of an insurance business	
Skills possessed	**Skills required**
Strategy setting	Coaching people
Picking the right people	Motivating people
Networking with the investors	Championing change
Problem solving	Communicating effectively
	Commercial awareness

In order to develop the skills, choose an option that suits your style. For instance, ask a trusted confidant to help you develop a management development plan; seek out and talk to fellow entrepreneurs who have been through a similar development experience; or book yourself on a business-skills development programme. Talk to your training department about the options or contact your local Business Link for advice on appropriate courses.

Developing top-management key business competencies

Assess yourself against these competencies, which have been developed by some highly successful European businesses. These are not 'the' management competencies but they are used by several businesses.

If you are really brave ask your team or colleague to complete it for you as well!

Qualities	Very false – very true
1. LEADERSHIP: Leading an effective team to produce results beyond expectations	
Develops a shared purpose across the business	1 2 3 4 5
Creates an environment that inspires people to excel	1 2 3 4 5
Is an inspirational role model	1 2 3 4 5
2. COMMUNICATION: Encouraging understanding by communication effectively	
Actively promotes the company externally	1 2 3 4 5
Encourages open communication and feedback	1 2 3 4 5
Ensures everybody is clear about their roles, the business's aims and key issues	1 2 3 4 5

Qualities	Very false – very true
3. COMMERCIAL AWARENESS: Considering costs and profits in all activities and decisions	
Ensures people's actions are commercial at all times	1 2 3 4 5
Constantly picks up opportunities and threats	1 2 3 4 5
Keeps abreast of customer and competitor trends and activity	1 2 3 4 5
4. CHANGE ORIENTATION: Implementing change to drive business improvement	
Creates an environment where people continually improve the business	1 2 3 4 5
Constantly challenges existing process and thinking	1 2 3 4 5
Champions change in the business	1 2 3 4 5
5. WORKING WITH OTHERS: Collaborating with others to improve business performance	
Promotes open communication and collaboration	1 2 3 4 5
Creates a climate that promotes honesty, openness and integrity	1 2 3 4 5
Promotes cross-functional team working	1 2 3 4 5
6. DEVELOPING PEOPLE: Creating opportunities to develop self and others	
Demonstrates the importance of people development throughout the business	1 2 3 4 5
Makes training and development a way of life in the business	1 2 3 4 5
Acts as a role model by developing self	1 2 3 4 5
7. TAKING RESPONSIBILITY: Resolving issues and delivering solutions	
Ensures top team focus on key strategic priorities	1 2 3 4 5
Takes personal responsibility for the design and delivery of the strategy	1 2 3 4 5
Ensures top team accept shared responsibility for complex business decisions	1 2 3 4 5
8. PRACTICAL THINKING: Seeking and finding pragmatic solutions	
Creates innovative solutions to complex issues	1 2 3 4 5
Is good at problem solving	1 2 3 4 5
Ensures a flow of good ideas get turned into business-improvement actions	1 2 3 4 5

Qualities	Very false – very true
9. PLANNING: Formulating actions to achieve objectives	
Ensures everybody is clear about how these roles fit with the business plan	1 2 3 4 5
Develops a continuous improvement culture into the plan	1 2 3 4 5
Ensures agreed actions are implemented successfully	1 2 3 4 5
10. QUALITY FOCUS: Continually improving standards	
Benchmarks company performance	1 2 3 4 5
Ensures consistent achievement of company standards	1 2 3 4 5
Ensures managers review and improve quality	1 2 3 4 5

Interpreting your scores

Scores of 4 or 5 would be regarded as strengths. Scores of 1 or 2 would probably be regarded as weaknesses. A score of 3 would be average.

Which of these competencies do you really need to deliver your strategy? Are they currently strengths? Which do you need to develop?

List here your development needs, based on your analysis of your scores and your business needs right now.

1. ....

2. ....

3. ....

4. ....

5. ....

Talk to someone you trust about your needs.
Start doing something – anything ...

Hire a personal coach

Fitness fanatics have been hiring personal coaches and trainers for years to help them get their bodies in shape. This often proves a good investment.

Have you thought about hiring a personal coach to help you get your management skills in shape? This is a fast-growing trend in the business world today. Those who have used a coach often report significant gains in confidence and competence.

Investigate hiring a personal coach if this suits your needs and style. Contact the Institute of Management Consultancy on 020 7242 2140 for details of accredited personal coaches. Ask around in order to find out who the good coaches are in your area. For American and Australian coaches, log on to www.google.com and enter 'executive coaching' (for the US) or 'executive coaching australia'. This will give you a number of contacts.

Some typical reasons for hiring a coach

- New into a role – need development.
- Help to manage 'difficult people'.
- To take a more strategic perspective.
- To challenge and change a culture.
- To manage a new and/or difficult project.
- To become more assertive in managing people.
- To develop leadership skills.

Actions to take:

1. ....
2. ....
3. ....

> TIP: Have a go at toolkit 3 'Developing your personal qualities' – it complements this one.

Toolkit 3 – Developing your personal qualities

- Develop your creative and innovative skills.
- Reduce stress and achieve inner calm.
- Improve your health and increase your energy levels.

Toolkit 2, 'Developing your business skills', focused upon developing traditional business skills. This toolkit helps you to nurture and develop your personal qualities. Several studies highlight the difference between business skills and personal qualities:

Business skills – example (left-brain)	Personal qualities – example (right-brain)
Planning	Coping with stress and risk
Profit planning	Being persistent
Problem solving	Obsessive commitment
Decision making	Taking responsibility
Developing strategy	Being innovative and creative

Traditional (left-brain) business skills can be taught and learned. The term 'left-brain' refers to the systematic, rational, detailed, planning functions of the brain. Personal (right-brain) qualities are the creative, intuitive side of the brain. These cannot be taught using traditional teaching methods. So how do you develop personal qualities?

We now know that entrepreneurs develop their personal qualities in four distinctive ways. These can be contrasted with the traditional ways of teaching business skills:

Traditional ways of learning business skills (left brain)	Entrepreneurs' preferred ways of developing their personal qualities (right brain)
By reading business books	By doing the job i.e. by trial and error
Attending training courses	Learning from successful entrpreneurs like themselves
Being formally taught by business experts	Working with members of their own team
	Talking with their family and friends

You will see that the ways people develop personal qualities are largely informal, unplanned and therefore there is a chance that these skills are never properly developed. Here are some ways to develop some of them. Clearly, these are not all the qualities you need, but they do appear often in papers and articles on personal business qualities.

Step 1: Assess your personal strengths and weaknesses

Rate yourself on these personal qualities: 1 = very poor, 10 = outstanding. Be honest with your rating, there is no point in fooling yourself.

Quality	Score
Being creative	1 2 3 4 5 6 7 8 9 10
Being determined and persistent	1 2 3 4 5 6 7 8 9 10
Being willing to be flexible	1 2 3 4 5 6 7 8 9 10
Being highly opportunistic	1 2 3 4 5 6 7 8 9 10
Having a 'can do' attitude	1 2 3 4 5 6 7 8 9 10
Being very risk-conscious	1 2 3 4 5 6 7 8 9 10
Being very focused	1 2 3 4 5 6 7 8 9 10
Thinking strategically	1 2 3 4 5 6 7 8 9 10
Having obsessive commitment	1 2 3 4 5 6 7 8 9 10
Accepting responsibility	1 2 3 4 5 6 7 8 9 10
Being willing to cope with uncertainty and stress	1 2 3 4 5 6 7 8 9 10
Believing in your own capability	1 2 3 4 5 6 7 8 9 10
Networking with people	1 2 3 4 5 6 7 8 9 10

Making sense of your scores

From 1–3 would be regarded as a low score, which you might need to develop. Can anyone else in your team cover you on this factor? From 4–7 are average scores – maybe a strength or a weakness, depending upon your circumstances. Scores from 8–10 would be strengths. However, too high a score can also cause problems. For instance, a 10 on obsessive commitment may lead to problems in your personal life: you could be a workaholic, for example.

Step 2: Some ways to develop your personal qualities

Transcendental meditation

There is a growing body of scientific evidence that shows that transcendental meditation (TM) can really help to develop some personal qualities. The benefit is that the development of these critical personal qualities becomes less of a lottery. Here are two examples of how TM has been put to use:

1. South India Research Institute Ltd

South India Research Institute Ltd (SIRIS) comprises sixteen industries manufacturing basic chemicals, pharmaceuticals, pesticides and edible oils. A large majority of employees practise transcendental meditation. After implementing the TM programme, G S Raju, chairman of the corporation, noted: 'Transcendental meditation is practised during working hours twenty minutes twice a day. Apart from improving performance, this has helped the progress of the company. Workers now work only seven hours but produce ten hours' worth of output. Before learning transcendental meditation, in eight hours of work the productivity was equivalent to only six hours – an increase of productivity by fifty-seven per cent. In addition, there was a marked reduction in stress, reduced absenteeism, and the workers reported less fatigue, worries and anxiety.'

2. Sumitomo Heavy Industries

More than ten thousand businesspeople in Japan have learned the transcendental meditation technique. Over two thousand of them are top executives of leading Japanese companies, including Sumitomo Heavy Industries, Toyota Motor Company and One World Supermarkets. Over a hundred Japanese companies have introduced the TM programme to their managers and employees.

Participants showed substantial improvements in physical and mental health, including significant reductions in anxiety, insomnia, depression, emotional instability, physical complaints, smoking and digestive problems. Here are some personal statements:

Burton A Dole Jr, former chairman and CEO of Puritan Bennett Corp., a leading manufacturer of respiratory products, says, 'The key to success in today's world is innovation, creativity – beyond anything else. If you create products and services that are clearly better than what your competitors produce, you're going to succeed. Having the ability to enhance one's own creativity as well as that of one's employees seems to me to be the ultimate responsibility of a manager within a company. And the transcendental meditation programme allows that creativity enhancement to take place beyond anything I've ever seen.'

Steve Rubin, chairman and CEO of United Fuels International Inc., an international energy brokerage firm, has this to say: 'After meditating I have the mental clarity and alertness for laser focus on the details and, at the same time, for broad comprehension so I don't get lost in the details. I find myself continuously growing in insight and intuition, as well as in the ability to focus and analyse. Over my years in business, the TM technique has been a real competitive advantage.'

Sir John Harvey-Jones, former chairman of ICI, says, 'I thoroughly recommend from personal experience TM to anyone running a business in today's highly stressful world.'

Story – TM: A Personal Experience

My work with entrepreneurs revealed the need to find a way to help them to develop their personal qualities. Traditional business teaching methods do not develop personal qualities.

I was discussing this problem with a business friend who then told me that he started TM on the advice of his doctor in order to reduce his blood pressure. He found that, at the same time, his creativity had increased, and he felt less stressed. He said he was able to work harder without feeling tired and to think more clearly. This sounded like an avenue worth pursuing, so I signed myself up as a guinea pig to test the effects of TM. Had I discovered a solution by accident? I was a bit sceptical but I enrolled on a TM programme in Sheffield, and within three months my blood pressure had reduced, I felt less stressed and people told me I was much more relaxed. In fact one person said I'd started looking happy.

This was not the reason I attended the programme but I was delighted with the unexpected bonus of the personal benefits!

I can recommend TM from personal experience and that's why it is included in this book. TM can help you to develop the personal qualities necessary to survive and prosper in today's world.

How does TM work?

I experienced right from the beginning that TM had a very settling effect on my mind. I noticed, too, that physical activity settled down in just the same way. The whole system became very quiet.

This is the secret of TM: rest. It gives very deep rest to mind and body – some scientists say it's deeper than the deepest sleep. And when people are rested they're happier, healthier and more creative. They learn better. They respond to stress more positively. They enjoy coming into work in the morning. One of the selling points of TM in the US has been as a cost-effective way of retaining staff. Corporations know that every time they have to replace an executive it costs them $250,000 plus. To pay for an employee's TM course costs them $1,000 (£500 in the UK is the standard course fee. If you want the teacher to come to you on site it will cost more.)

Is TM any different?

Like me, you've probably noticed recently that there's been a lot in the Sunday papers about meditation and complementary therapies generally. There's usually a line in them that goes something like this: 'Recent research shows that meditation can be a valuable tool in coping with stress.' Such statements have made Dr Jaan Suurkula very cross. So much so that he's just set up his own website, Swedish Physicians for Transcendental Meditation. Dr Suurkula explains:

> Practically all the research proving that meditation is beneficial has been done on TM. Yet people are commonly saying that all kinds of meditation are essentially as beneficial. This has no scientific basis and is due to ignorance about the great differences between mediation techniques.

You can visit his site at http://home.swipnet.se/tmdoctors/ptm.htm

Even though TM is a very ancient technique and has remained unchanged for thousands of years, the instruction course, which takes four consecutive days for a couple of hours each day, is now structured in an easy, practical way for businesspeople.

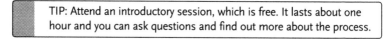

TIP: Attend an introductory session, which is free. It lasts about one hour and you can ask questions and find out more about the process.

To find out more about transcendental meditation, contact the TM UK Centre on 08705 143733 or email: info@t-m.org.uk; for the US log on to www.tm.org, or www.tm.org.au for Australia. You can request an information pack, and they will send you details of your nearest TM centre. Ask them to send you the video in which professionals and businesspeople introduce TM.

If you want to read more about TM you can visit the website at www.t-m.org.uk. It summarises over 150 scientific papers on the benefits of TM as researched around the world.

Clearly TM will help you to develop some of these personal qualities. But how do you develop others such as:

- being focused
- thinking strategically
- being willing to cope with uncertainty
- networking with people

Here are some ideas, which might help:

Try using the 'Tools for prioritising and focusing' (Toolkit 6). These will help you to get focus and direction into your life and work.

Toolkit 9, 'Redoing your strategy in order to revitalise your business', will help you think strategically. One technique I learned from Dick Watson of Keepmoat PLC was to write down my three or four strategic priorities on a card and carry it with me at all times. This kept reminding me to stay focused on the strategic issues.

Simon Woodroffe of Yo Sushi has developed a simple but very effective way of handling situations where he had little experience or confidence, for example, asking his bank for funding or getting to see key people. He calls it 'Act as if …' 'I just act as if it's no big deal and appear confident, hopefully not arrogant; in many cases I got what I want.' If you face new situations try acting as if … and see if it works for you.

Dinah Bennett of Durham Business School taught me a key lesson in networking. I was happy running workshops and talking to people with my props, such as overhead projector and flipchart. Yet when I went into a room of strangers to network I got nervous. Dinah told me that everybody else was probably even more nervous than I was. But if you bite the bullet and introduce yourself to people your confidence grows, she said. It did and I found that networking was a fantastic business development process. Try using 'Build your business by networking' toolkit 20.

Summary

Personal qualities are critical to success in business. They can't be taught but they can be developed. As your confidence and personal qualities develop, so does your business – and that's the payoff.

Toolkit 4 – being interpersonally skilled

- Build strong relationships.
- Get buy-in to your plans.
- Inspire people.

The skill of being able to deal effectively with people at all levels has been shown in many studies to be a key skill for successful businesspeople.

Whether it's motivating a team, selling to key customers, getting buy-in from stakeholders, talking up the share price in the city or simply getting the best out of people; good interpersonal skills separate the real leaders from the pack.

Story – A Tale of Two Bosses

When I first started my career at Steetley PLC my boss was an former air vice-marshal.

He could not remember my name, so he called me John. When it came to the annual appraisal (which I looked forward to) he often cancelled our meeting at the last moment.

'Fill in the form, John,' he would say. 'I'm too busy.'

Consequently he got 100 per cent out of me: 10 per cent on Mondays, 20 per cent on Tuesdays ...

Tony Kitson was my next boss. At the annual appraisal he would prepare for it very carefully. He would give me two to three hours, when we would talk about my career. He was enthusiastic, encouraging and very supportive. He encouraged me to do an MBA, giving me time off to study. He remembered all my children's birthdays. He would call me up prior to board meetings and ask for my advice and help. He was a real turning point in my career and confidence.

Tony had the interpersonal skills to inspire everybody, including shareholders, customers, his board, colleagues and even my children.

I have not seen Tony for 25 years, but, if he called me tomorrow and asked me to go to London for him, my response would be, 'Tony, do you want me to run there with a sack of coal on my back ...?' That's the point: one boss was self-orientated and the other could get people to walk on water for him.

The difference? Interpersonal skills.

Seven components of interpersonal skills

1. Listening

■ Listen with respect, interest and total attention.

■ Maintain eye contact at all times.

■ Do not interrupt or end people's sentences for them: let them finish.

- Leave space for people to talk by staying quiet.
- Don't offer solutions or opinions too early.
- Provide encouragement and support.

2. Showing support

- Practise a five-to-one ratio of support to criticism.
- Avoid 'Yes but ...'.
- Avoid telling them your problems – it does not create empathy, but only annoys people.

3. Allowing time

- Give people time to talk – don't rush or slow down the pace of the discussion.

4. Control of your body language

- Be careful to keep your body language in step with your purpose: for example, don't cross your arms if you want to appear open and inclusive.
- Be relaxed and smile in order to encourage people to talk.

5. Providing information at the right time

- Disclose things about yourself to show you are human; show that you can be self-deprecating.
- Sometimes people do need information, but don't overload them: provide it at the right time.

6. Asking helpful questions

Helpful questions are those that make a positive assumption and direct the speaker's attention back to their goal. Here are some examples:

- If you were the manager what issues would you tackle first and how would you do it?
- If you knew you were critical to the organisation's success, how would you approach your work?
- If you knew that you were as smart as your boss, how would you present yourself to her or him?

7. Equality

> ■ Treat the person as a peer or a friend.
> ■ Give equal opportunities to talk and listen.
> ■ Keep to boundaries.

Using these skills builds rapport and empathy in most interpersonal situations. People want to do business with people they trust and like, and these skills have proved important in building relationships with people.

You may have noticed that often women possess these skills. Sometimes men (including me) need to work at their interpersonal skills because of their conditioning and the role models they follow:

Good interpersonal skills	Male conditioning
Listen	Interrupt, talk over, compete for air space
Ask helpful questions	Give advice
Establish equality	Assume superiority
Encourage	Compete
Appreciate	Criticise

The good news is that interpersonal skills can be developed.

Step 1: Assessing your levels of interpersonal skills

Are you interested in how you rate on these key interpersonal skills?

If you are, then photocopy the interpersonal-skills assessment below and ask selected people to fill it in, in order to give you some feedback. This will raise your consciousness level and help you take stock of what you need to do in order to improve your interpersonal skills. Low scores may explain why you are not getting the results from people you desire.

Interpersonal-skills assessment

Name (person being assessed): _____

Name of Assessor: _____

Please answer these following questions as honestly as you possibly can. Your feedback will help your colleague.

Qualities	Rating	
	Low/poor	High/excellent
1. Really listens carefully with respect and interest		1 2 3 4 5 6 7 8 9 10
2. Asks good questions rather than gives opinions		1 2 3 4 5 6 7 8 9 10
3. Treats everybody equally		1 2 3 4 5 6 7 8 9 10
4. Practices a 5:1 ratio of appreciation to criticism		1 2 3 4 5 6 7 8 9 10
5. Encourages and collaborates rather than competes		1 2 3 4 5 6 7 8 9 10
6. Gives space and time for open discussions		1 2 3 4 5 6 7 8 9 10
7. Appears to be honest and straightforward		1 2 3 4 5 6 7 8 9 10
8. Communicates very clearly with people		1 2 3 4 5 6 7 8 9 10
9. Shows empathy, interest and understanding		1 2 3 4 5 6 7 8 9 10
10. Is assertive rather than aggressive or passive		1 2 3 4 5 6 7 8 9 10
Total:		_____

Reviewing your scores

80% + Well done. You will be producing outstanding results through people. You have an excellent range of interpersonal skills.

60% + Average for managers and leaders. Where do you need to improve? How can you develop your skills above 60%?

40% + Below average. A lot of work to do. Maybe you should think of undertaking some formal training in interpersonal skills.

20% + Are you in the right job? Maybe you should be a lighthouse keeper or a shepherd.

Step 2: Developing your interpersonal skills

Here are some actions you can take to develop your low scores on the assessment:

- Book yourself on a good-quality interpersonal-skills development programme.
- Hire a personal coach to help you to develop your skills.

- Copy good role models who are highly competent at the skills you want to develop.

- Practise, practise, practise: practise the skill you want to develop in real-life situations.

- Ask for feedback: ask selected people to give you honest feedback on whether your skills are improving. Do they notice a difference? For example, ask people to give you feedback on how well you manage meetings.

- Act as if … Just do it. Act as if you were already interpersonally skilled and you will develop.

- Write out a plan on a piece of card and keep it with you. Top sports people use this technique all the time to keep them focused.

- Read a good book on the subject: e.g., Gavin Kennedy's book *Everything is Negotiable*.

- Ask people to share their way of using a particular skill, such as showing interest. Integrate the best ideas into your skill set.

- Show humility, not arrogance.

TIP: If you want to build real rapport and trust with people, then be authentic at all times. This means putting into words what you are seeing or feeling. For instance, you could say, 'You look a bit puzzled, what are you thinking about?' Or 'This doesn't feel right to me – how are you feeling right now?' This is a very powerful way of building rapport and trust.

Step 3: Role modelling

We created this approach to help people to develop their interpersonal skills because we found that traditional training courses were not effective. This approach works by getting a team of four to six people together who want to develop their interpersonal skills (including you).

The approach also is a good team-building exercise.

Process	Notes
1. Invite people to work on improving their interpersonal skills.	
2. The ground rules are that there should be no analysis of rights or wrongs.	

Process	Notes
3. A volunteer in the group starts the process by naming an interpersonal episode they would like to develop.	An episode is a short interaction, for instance, asking questions in selling or giving difficult feedback in appraisals.
	People do not have problems with total interpersonal situations such as selling. They usually are good at some parts (episodes), such as dealing with objections in the sales process, and have problems with others, such as asking for the order.
4. The volunteer demonstrates how they currently perform the episode with another person. For instance, volunteer tries asking questions in a sales situation. Another member of the team acts as a typical buyer. The episode usually lasts for two to three minutes.	Authenticity check. Check after one minute whether the role-play is the same as the real situation.
	Nobody is allowed to comment, for instance, to say that was poor or they wouldn't do it like that. No discussion: just role-play.
5. Another group member offers to demonstrate how they deal with the same episode.	There are always people in the group who are skilled and can demonstrate the episode really well.
The original group member is asked to notice how their colleague does it.	
6. Step 5 is repeated with another group member demonstrating how they do it.	No discussion or evaluation is allowed.
7. The original problem owner is then asked to pick bits of what they have seen that they want to incorporate into their approach (Steps 5–6) and repeat the episode.	
8. Congratulate the individual on their development. The difference between Steps 4–7 will be obvious to everyone.	
Repeat Steps 3–9 with other members of the group, dealing with their interpersonal skill problems.	An added bonus is to video Steps 4 and 9, the before and after, to capture the skill development.

Role modelling has been used by many people to develop:

- sales skills
- interviewing skills
- presentation skills
- appraisal skills
- skills in running a meeting
- sales management skills
- coaching skills

It works because people like to learn from their peers. They learn by watching what others do and copying. The lack of criticism ensures that a positive learning environment is created where people are happy to experiment and learn.

Try it. It works because it's simple and fun, and is in line with how people prefer to develop interpersonal skills.

Toolkit 5 – Providing leadership

- Produce results beyond expectations.
- Create a turned on team.
- Build a better business.

The purpose of this toolkit is to help leaders to inspire their teams in order to change and develop the business together.

But first a few key principles.

First, the stance that really effective leaders take is that they are there to serve their people and not to be served themselves. This is so critical I am going to repeat it: *The stance that really effective leaders take is that they are there to serve their people and not to be served themselves.* They understand that abuse of position and a command-and-control culture cannot deliver results beyond expectations. You need to engage hearts and minds. Leaders invert the traditional business pyramid.

Traditional Business	*Leadership*
Leader	Team

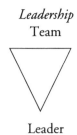

Followers	Leader

In the traditional business model the followers wait for the leaders to be told what to do. This model relies on three or four leaders providing all the ideas. In other words, leaders think, followers follow. This separation of thinking from working has proved to be highly inefficient.

In stark contrast, the leadership model encourages everybody in the organisation to think and act on behalf of the business. The Japanese call this *kaizen*, which means continuous improvement by everybody all the time. If you are competing with a business in which a hundred brains are constantly striving to improve the business and you are operating out of the traditional business model, you will have real problems keeping up with them.

This is a critical mind shift for leaders to make. This toolkit will help you make the change.

The next key principle is that management and leadership are different roles. *Managers* make the business work effectively by hitting agreed targets and achieving profit margins and delivery plans and so forth. Managers meet expectations. *Leaders* make the business better. They exceed expectations by engaging everybody to challenge and change it. Leaders produce results beyond expectations.

Story – CompuAdd Computers

Martin Vincent, CEO of the computer manufacturer CompuAdd, attended a presentation of Toolkit 5, 'Providing leadership', in Bristol in 1995. His business had sales of £12 million with a loss of £200,000.

He knew he had to do something to improve the performance of his business; he also knew he needed to provide the leadership to make it happen.

Martin got his team together and they established a vision

using Toolkit 8, 'Creating a vision for your business'. 'I am a typical accountant,' said Martin, 'so I didn't find leading the team in a creative, visioning exercise a natural process, but the "Vision" toolkit helped because it gave me a framework.'

The vision involved becoming a £15 million profitable business by creating long-term partnerships with large customers.

'We then did Steps 2 and 3 in the toolkit together by identifying as a team the blockages to the delivery of the vision. This provided us with an excellent agenda for change. We all knew what we had to do. I followed the advice in the toolkit and led a project myself on improving our deliveries on time.

'We had a really tough time. Unfortunately, two directors had to leave and morale was very up and down. I had to keep people going through these tough times. Part of our problem was people were frightened to try things and make mistakes because they were in fear of their own jobs. I found that I actually enjoyed being the leader, encouraging, supporting and helping my people.'

Martin assigned each of the blockages as a 'project' to one of his directors or senior managers with a brief to remove them. He took the precaution of restructuring his board over a period of six months to improve competence and commitment. 'We had a dramatic success, and we have significantly improved our profits every year for the past three years.'

Martin sold CompuAdd to a competitor in 1999 for a healthy profit.

The third key principle is to be honest with your people. The key marketing principle is giving your customers what they want. Numerous studies show that employees want their leaders to be:

- honest – 'Tell it as it is – no spin ...'
- forward-looking – 'What's the vision?'
- inspirational – 'Motivate me to do my best'
- competent as leaders – 'They produced the promised results'

So, if that's what employees want, then, following the marketing mantra, leaders should provide it. Here's how to do it:

Step 1: An inspirational vision

Get your team together and develop an inspirational vision or common purpose (see Toolkit 8). This should provide focus and direction for everyone in the business. Make sure there is something in the vision for employees, customers and investors.

For example, in three years' time we will have:

- grown by 50 per cent in sales
- developed three new products
- enabled all staff to share in our business
- produced returns to investors in the top 20 per cent for our industry

> TIP: Ask questions, get people contributing their ideas – they must not all be yours ...

Step 2: Visionary ideas

Ask people to contribute ideas to how the vision can be achieved (see Toolkit 7, 'Working on the business'). Develop a process to ensure a continuous flow of vision delivery ideas, such as monthly brainstorming sessions or working on the business teams.

Step 3: Remove blockages

Are there any blockages to the delivery of the vision. One way of generating ideas that will help deliver the vision is to ask the questions:

- What's stopping us achieving our vision?
- What do we have to get better at in order to deliver our vision?

Step 4: Ideas into projects

Turn the best ideas that emerge from Steps 2 and 3 into projects. Pick project leaders and agree objectives (this is the *what*). For instance, to set up a business-generating system in order to get us into new markets by 31.3.2003; to design a system that we can run internally.

> TIP: Make sure you lead one project yourself – this sends a powerful message: 'We are in this together.'

Step 5: Get buy-in to the projects

Allow the project leaders to produce action plans for the projects (this is the *how*). (See example action plan below.) Support them, encourage them and give them ownership, responsibility and accountability.

Example action plan

Objectives

1. To set up a business generating system in order to get us into new markets by 31.3.03.
2. To design a system which can be run internally.

Plan

1. Set up a small internal team to develop the system, including sales, production and customer-service representatives, by 1.2.02.
2. Identify current conversion rates, for example, leads to enquiries to orders, in the key market sectors by 1.3.02.
3. Analyse effectiveness of current marketing methods by 18.3.02.
4. Establish average order size in key markets by 30.3.02.
5. Calculate sales required monthly in each market sector by 6.4.02.
6. Establish new business-generating system to create required sales levels by 1.5.02.
7. Pilot and test the system for three months by 1.8.02.
8. Evaluate and roll out the system by 1.9.02.
9. Train all staff to operate the new system by 1.10.02.

TIP: Ask for one-page plans – this allows them to do the thinking but also allows you to sign them off and sleep easy in your bed.

Step 6: Create a climate of learning

- Tell them you want them to make lots of mistakes.
- Tell them it's OK to experiment and try things.
- Celebrate failure, laugh at it and move on.

An example not to follow ...

A CEO called me up one day and said he could not get his team to experiment, take risks and learn. I visited his operation and sat in on a typical day with him.

He delegated a project to a team member. He seemed to follow the classical delegation routine i.e., agree objectives, explain the project, make resources available, be supportive etc.

I could not understand why he had a problem with his team. Right at the end, as the individual stood up to leave, the CEO bellowed at him 'John don't screw it up...'!

Not a climate of learning ...

Step 7: Help them to be persistent in adversity

- Keep encouraging them to keep going, particularly when the going gets tough.
- Roll your sleeves up and lend a hand, but don't take over.

TIP: Order the pizza and drinks if the teams are working late. Show them how much you appreciate their efforts.

Step 8: Celebrate success
Do this loudly and publicly!

Toolkit 6: Tools for prioritising and focusing

- Work smarter, not harder.
- Focus on the important issues.
- Manage your time and energies effectively.

In an increasingly competitive and busy business world, it's very easy to rush around trying to be all things to all people. Downsizing and the long-hours culture, which have developed over the past five years, have exacerbated this problem.

The top management job is to work on the strategic and important issues for the business. Managers also need to spend time working *on* as well as working *in* the business (see Toolkit 7).

So, as the CEO or MD, you need to prioritise and focus on those parts of the business that need your attention.

Here are some tools that managers have found helpful in bringing focus and direction to their work. You can use them and you can encourage your top team to use them.

1. Strategic priorities

Complete the following:

Our strategy/plan calls for..
(cost reduction, improving market share, building our brands, delighting customers, etc.).

Therefore I should be focusing upon...................................
(whatever it is) right now.

Or …

Our strategy calls for........................ and I have been spending the last month on..................... (review your diary). Therefore, have I got my priorities right?

2. Focus

Answer the following question on a scale of 1–100% (1 being very poor, 100 being perfect): What chances of success does our plan currently have? Or: How happy are we with our business?

Say your answer is 65%, then ask: What do we need to do right now to move from 65 to 100%? What's blocking our progress?

List your answers and focus upon them.

To maintain short-term focus try cutting your plans to one sheet of paper, the five or six key points. This could be for a meeting, a workshop, a project or a visit to a business unit.

John McEnroe, ranked as the number-one best men's tennis player in the world for four years running (1981–4), used to write down his game plan for each tennis game he played. He referred to it sometimes during the game because he found that his plans and focus could go out of the window in the heat of the battle.

Staying focused is key in sport. It's also key in business.

3. Top team priorities

Get your top team together and undertake this simple but potentially very powerful exercise:

 ■ Tell them you want to ensure that you're all focused on the right priorities for the business.

- Ask them to write down individually, without conferring, what they perceive the top three priorities for the business are for the next twelve months.
- Now ask them to write down, without conferring, what their three key priorities are for the next twelve months.
- Finally, ask them to write down what they believe your three priorities should be for the next twelve months.

Now share this information in order to clarify (a) the business priorities, (b) the individual focus and (c) your focus.

> TIP: When you share the information guard against people rationalising with, 'We have all got just about the same priorities, haven't we?' The answer to that is usually no.

Sometimes when this exercise has been done the differences between individual perceptions are so great that you think you are looking at different businesses! But that's the point of doing it: to get focus and direction in your team's efforts.

If you really want to go deeper with this one, when people say, 'We are focused on the priorities already', ask them: 'What projects are you currently working on that focus on these priorities right now?' Then say, 'Let's review our discussion honestly together and see how much time we are actually giving these priorities. Let's review and discuss. If necessary go back through each other's diary together.'

Light the blue touch paper and stand back!

4. Play to strengths

Ask yourself 'What am I good at?' 'What do I really enjoy doing?' Now review how you have actually spent your time in the last three months. Don't guess: go through your diary.

What do you learn from this review? Refocus on your strengths and delegate your weaknesses to other people.

Example

> I am an ideas person who enjoys seeing the big picture and spotting opportunities. I am poor at detail and following things through to completion.
>
> Therefore I need a good PA who ensures the detail gets done and partners who are finishers to get projects completed on time.

5. Search for the domino

A very powerful way to prioritise actions is to search and focus on the domino. The *domino*? Well, if you line dominoes up on their edge and space them an inch (2.5cm) apart and then knock over the end domino the rest tumble down in order. So one action has an impact on lots of others.

If you have a list of ideas or important actions try to find the domino – the one matter that, if fixed or resolved, will have a major impact on a number of others.

Example

A global chemical company wanted to develop its business. It used several toolkits to identify opportunities, including Toolkit 16 ('Conducting a customer perception survey'), Toolkit 28 ('Fixing system slippage') and Toolkit 19 ('Build your business by delighting customers').

A list of thirty improvement actions was identified. A debate with the management team identified their domino. They wanted to develop their business by selling more to existing customers, creating new customers and developing some new product applications.

The business sold through agents and distributors globally. Their agents also represented some of their competitors. They realised that if they built stronger links with the agents they could provide new leads, market information, product opportunities and perhaps even some competitor information. This one domino could have a real impact on a number of their key issues.

CHAPTER TWO

Working on the Business

Toolkit 7

Toolkit 7: Working on the business

- Significantly improve the performance of your business in all aspects.
- Use the wisdom within your business to develop it – it's free.
- Create a strong internal customer culture by removing blockages and disconnects internally.

This toolkit is important because it is a general-purpose one that can be used in conjunction with several of the others. It helps you to make significant changes to your business by dealing with the inertia and obstacles that usually block change, particularly in larger businesses.

The purpose of this toolkit is to harness the wisdom and energies of your people in order to improve the performance of your business by working *on* as well as *in* it.

Often managers are so busy working *in* the business, solving problems and putting out fires, that they feel unable to spend the time working *on* the business to improve it. The consequence is that they continue firefighting and the business performance stays exactly the same or deteriorates.

In order to work *on* the business and manage change effectively, the following short reading should get you into the right frame of mind. It is based upon the work of my friend Gerard Egan, who has successfully helped businesses all over the world to change over the past thirty years.

Understanding change – a short introduction

Change can be a messy process. Most people hate it, because it generally upsets their rhythm and even keeps them awake at night. Little wonder many resist it.

Many organisations also suffer from inertia and an inability to change, and suffer several types of malaise, including the 'silo syndrome', which is competition rather than co-operation between departments and the overburdening bureaucracy that stifles rather than liberates them. When they do change direction they find it very difficult to bring the prevailing culture in line with the demands of the new strategy.

It's no surprise to learn that 95 per cent of all the radical products and services developed over the past hundred years have come from businesses employing fewer than twenty people. That's the bad news. The good news is that, if you understand and manage the dynamics of change, then it is possible to deal with the worst effects of inertia, culture, turf wars, egos and internal politics.

Let's look at some change issues in more depth.

1. Eighty per cent of discretionary change initiatives are abandoned as failures within two years. Discretionary change is where people perceive they have a choice – so often people decide not to change and thus the change initiative fails.

However eighty per cent of nondiscretionary change initiatives succeed. 'We have no choice, this is serious, so let's get it done.'

So how do you position your change programmes as nondiscretionary change initiatives? This process of working *on* the business has been designed to do just that, so read on.

2. If you are to make change a success you need to deal with the blockages to the process. These are:

> ■ The top team believe that everybody needs to change but them ...
> ■ There is no process to empower people within the business to change.
> ■ People try to introduce the change through the existing command-and-control culture, which creates resistance.

This toolkit deals with these three blockages.

3. Very often the reward system sends the wrong messages to people: keep doing what you are doing. Therefore, if you want to change the culture, then change the reward system.

4. The principles to make change nondiscretionary, deal with the blockages and improve the business, therefore, are:

- Top management must get involved and be positive role models for the change. As my mentor, Gerard Egan, said, 'Watch their feet, not their lips.'

- You need to harness the creative energies of your people to help you make the change.

- Work with the people with energy and commitment. Don't try to change your dinosaurs from day one. They will either come on board or leave eventually.

- Make membership of the change teams a voluntary process. Get buy-in from volunteers.

- Make the change nondiscretionary. This could be done by **providing new information** to the team (one example is to conduct a customer survey and report the results – this is how bad we are!). You should also **create a vision** with them about how you want the future to be (excite them in the process). And **communicate clearly** the consequences to the business (and to the team) of not changing. For instance, say, 'If we beat £10 million profit I will put in place a share option scheme for everybody. If we don't then I will seriously consider the future for the business. That's not a threat: it's the honest truth.'

- Change the reward systems in line with the change (e.g., 'If we beat £20 million profit I will share 20 per cent of everything over that with the team').

TIP: Do not keep the reward system the same regardless of performance. Senior managers get their perks and rewards regardless of performance in some businesses, therefore change is seen as discretionary and does not happen.

Let's look at a live example of working on the business:

Story – Ipswich Town Football Club

Ipswich Town Football Club uses the Toolkit 7 approach with all its staff, excluding players. At the first meeting when we used the toolkit, David Sheepshanks, the chairman, led off and got the whole thing going. He had fifty people split up into six cross-departmental teams.

The first session produced a staggering 60 improvement actions; some 24 were chosen as the most promising, and within a month 16 of these ideas had been put to the test and found to work – a success rate of 66 per cent (16 out of 24).

Now, 20 of the 50 commercial staff meet monthly to identify problems, come up with possible solutions, and then test out whether they work. The results are presented to the management group, which sanctions the changes needed. In 1998 the aim has been to improve customer service generally and to improve takings through 'cross selling' the services offered by the club. The use of the restaurant bar and function rooms has shot up. At the same time, the drive for sponsorship has been stepped up and many more season tickets have been sold than before. Ipswich Town Football Club has a set target of 80 per cent successful implementation and already it is well on the way to achieving it.

Here's how to work on *your* business:

Step 1: Assemble the team

Get your people together. Explain that you are going to work as a team to revitalise, build, improve, change (pick your own word) the business and tell them that they are all invited to participate.

You are not calling in experts or consultants. You believe that the wisdom is within to improve the business and you are going to do it together as a team. This initial meeting takes half a day.

Step 2: Identifying potential improvement

Suggest the team break into groups of 4–6 people of mixed departments and disciplines. Let them decide the composition of the groups, but try to ensure that the 'cliques' don't work together. Provide them with a flipchart or large piece of paper and pens. Join a team as a member but don't lead it.

Tell them it would be a great start if they could identify twenty areas for improving the business. Tell them to identify:

 things that they can personally take responsibility for improving: e.g., getting three quotes when purchasing

- team actions: e.g., setting up an intranet to share good ideas
- interteam issues: e.g., implementing an internal customer charter

Encourage them to avoid external undoable factors such 'exchange rates in Korea' or the old classic, 'if only management would …'

Try to provide some live examples: e.g., 'Fred suggested we staff reception over the lunch break to improve customer service. I thought that was a great idea!'

Ask them to write their ideas on the flipchart or paper. Make it fun. Act as a cheerleader. Now discuss and apply the rules of brainstorming:

- allow no finger pointing
- treat each other with respect
- be really honest
- take the actions you agree to
- get the facts – no guessing
- have positive can-do attitudes
- make it fun and exciting – an adventure, not a trauma

Example

This is part of the Brainstorm List of Ipswich Town Football Club:

- Sell services of restaurant, membership etc. at half-time via loudspeaker.
- Move ticket sales booths to better position (under cover).
- Get department managers to present their services to each other in order to increase knowledge of cross selling.
- Include all products and services, including contacts, in a special programme to 'keep by your phone'.
- Sell restaurant facilities for special events, including birthdays.
- Improve access to merchandising shop – six days a week.
- Employ telesales team to sell 'services to season-ticket holders'.

Step 3: Swap ideas
Get each team to present their ideas quickly to each other. Congratulate everybody. Sometimes people do not have all the data,

so they may need to do some further research or investigations. Encourage this process.

Step 4: Moving forward

Ask the teams how they want to take their ideas forward. Give them permission to take actions.

Step 5: The follow-up – some rules

Agree some ground rules for the follow-up. Here are some typical examples:

- Teams to prioritise the actions, since they cannot all be done at once.
- Whole group to meet again in one month's time to report on success and progress in implementing the ideas.
- Make sure you agree to undertake at least one action yourself. You are the boss and an important role model. You need to demonstrate your commitment to the process in actions, not just words.

TIP: If necessary, ask teams to produce a simple action plan for you to review – see the example in Toolkit 5, 'Providing leadership'.

Step 6: Implementation

The groups now implement their action plans. You offer support and help to remove any blockages. Show interest as they implement their plans.

Step 7: Reporting back

Groups report back to each other on progress one month later. Celebrate and reward success and learn lessons. Make it upbeat and positive, and say thank you and well done.

Calculate the percentage of actions successfully implemented against the total planned: e.g., 20 actions planned, 16 implemented = 80 per cent success rate. Anything over 80 per cent is an excellent score.

Make sure you complete your actions or else the whole thing will die before your eyes. Your challenge is to keep the action-taking above 80 per cent on a consistent basis.

Summary

Working on the business can create step changes. If you keep it going it can also change your culture into one of continuous improvement.

Troubleshooter

Potential problems	Suggested remedies
Too many issues get identified. You don't want to be seen as prescriptive in selecting ones to work upon.	1. Use a prioritising process i.e., voting. 2. Select some quick easy wins. 3. Pick some meaty ones and put others on the back burner for later on.
Actions are not taken: 'We are too busy ...'	1. Be assertive. Make attendance at the reviews non-discretionary. 2. Make sure you take your action as a role model.

CHAPTER THREE

Getting the Strategy Straight

Toolkits 8–10

Toolkit 8: Creating a vision for your business
Toolkit 9: Redoing your strategy in order to revitalise your business
Toolkit 10: Managing stakeholders effectively

Toolkit 8: Creating a vision for your business

- Provide focus and direction for everybody in your business.
- Enable your people to create the future you want.
- Harness the energy and commitment of all your people.

A vision is the picture of where you want your business to be at a specified time in the future. It is a key step in setting future strategy. Vision is much more than management jargon: it really does help to drive the business forward. The benefits that businesspeople report when they have had a clear vision include:

- 'Provided both energy and direction.'
- 'Helped guide our key decisions.'
- 'Challenged us to high levels of achievement.'
- 'Provided a common understanding of where our business is headed.'
- 'Enabled our people to work out how they could personally add value to our business.'

How to create a vision
The benefits of establishing a clear vision can be seen in the following story.

Story – A Management Consultancy

Ian Anderson took over as CEO of a consultancy in November 1990. His brief was to build the business from £1 million to £5 million profitability by 1995. He got the management team together and followed the principles in Toolkit 8, 'Creating a vision for your business'.

The initial brainstorm came up with lots of ideas and the team voted for the following five-year vision:

- no surprises for shareholders
- confident competent people
- delighted customers
- business expanded geographically
- reduced dependency on public-sector-funded work
- long-term partnerships with key customers
- all staff engaged in personal development
- minimum 5 per cent net profit
- joint product development with customers

The vision was adopted and then Step 2 in the toolkit was completed. This led to a Year One plan in order to deliver the vision:

- establishment of personal development plans for all staff
- a full-time networker being dispatched to Scotland to begin market development
- three joint research projects established with Training and Enterprise Councils on new products
- a consultancy business established targeting private clients (to reduce dependency on public sector)

'The lesson we learned was to ensure you prioritised your actions and then to allocate good people resources to it. Objectives without plans and resources don't work,' said Anderson.

The plan was successful in growing the business to £4.5 million sales by 1995. Unfortunately, the nature of the public-sector clients changed, which reduced the profitability. 'On reflection I would give us 80 per cent for implementation of the vision,' said Anderson, 'but the important thing was we learned invaluable lessons from the process and it certainly provided everybody with a clear focus and direction.'

Story – Keepmoat PLC

Fifteen years ago Keepmoat, a construction group, included 'Delight customers' as part of their vision. They set out to recruit marketing people with the remit of doing just that and included it in people's job guides, measured it monthly, built it into business plans and talked about it until it became part of the vocabulary of the business.

This took five years to build into the culture but has now become their competitive edge. Customers want to do business with them and they have become a leader in the market sector. So this was a success.

At the same time they decided that 'every person a businessperson' was part of the employee part of their vision and then did not do enough about it. Some of Keepmoat's people still had a building mindset instead of a business mindset. So some of the issues they currently face relate to the lack of business skills of some key people.

The difference between 'delighting customers' and 'every person a businessperson' was commitment and action planning. So one worked, one didn't.

The lessons for their business here are to try to get the balance of focus on customers, employees and stakeholders. Ignore one at your peril.

So how do you go about achieving this? Here's how:

Step 1: Assemble the team

Gather your team together. Tell them this is an opportunity for them to shape the future of the business. Select people who can add value to the process and whose buy-in is critical to your future success.

Provide flipcharts and pens. This helps in creating a shared process.

Agree a time frame for your vision that suits your business (e.g., three or five years into the future). You select the time frame that suits you.

Ask your people to address the following question (write it on the flipchart): 'If our organisation is to be really successful by meeting the true aspirations of our customers, our employees and our investors, what will have been accomplished in [X] years' time?'

There is a growing body of evidence that successful businesses seek to balance the interests of customers, employees and shareholders. Something for all the key stakeholders is a key principle in establishing a vision because then the stakeholders might support it.

Now list their answers on a flipchart.

Example – three-year vision

- We have delighted our customers.
- Our people have shared in our success.
- We have the best return on investment in our sector.
- We have built several strong key-customer partnerships.
- We have helped our people achieve their full potential.
- We have introduced three new successful products.
- We have a positive cash bank balance.
- Deliveries have constantly exceeded 98 per cent on time.
- Our succession plan process ensures we have strong internal candidates to fill key positions.
- We have a culture of continuous improvement.

Apply the rules of brainstorming from page 47.

> TIP: Write the aspirations in the present tense if they have been accomplished: e.g., '80% new business comes from referrals.'

Get the team to vote on or prioritise the aspirations. One way is to provide three green stickers – the type you get with wall planners – and let them each vote in any way they want for the best ideas. They can use three votes for one idea or two for one and one for a different idea or any other combination. This is a democratic prioritising method.

Count the number of votes – highest first, second highest second and so on. Aim for 6–8 vision statements. Now list the prioritised aspirations on a separate flipchart in priority order.

> TIP: You know the process is working well when the energy levels in the group increase during the process and people start getting excited, building on rather than disagreeing with each other's ideas.

This is now your first draft 3–5-year vision. Leave the process at this point, to allow time for reflection. Polish up the vision at a later date.

Ask your team: Does it excite people? Does it look challenging? Is it worth doing for everybody? However, a vision without a plan is a dream, so the next stage is to work out in Year 1 what needs to be done in order to move towards the 3–5-year picture.

Step 2: Listing actions

Put this question on a flipchart: 'If we are to move towards our vision, what do we need to accomplish in 12 months' time?' Get the team to list actions that need to have been accomplished, such as, 'Three-year vision: 80 per cent of new business comes from referrals. Therefore in twelve months we should have agreed our customer-delight process, and have a system in place to monitor the source of new enquiries.'

List the actions in the present tense. Build these actions into your next business plan and budgets. Bring them to life. Make sure you make somebody or a team responsible for each action. Communicate the vision as widely and as passionately as possible throughout your organisation, and talk about it enthusiastically at every opportunity.

Model the vision in your day-to-day activities. For instance, if your vision is to delight your customers, make sure you do all the things personally within your role that create delighted customers and ensure that your people see you do it.

Aim to win hearts and minds. Put the review of vision on regular meeting agendas. Celebrate and share success as you begin to achieve your vision.

Troubleshooter

Potential problems	Suggested remedies
Your vision is simply an extrapolation of the past.	Challenge the team to create a different future: 'How do we want it to be?' Let's worry about how we get there later. Vision is a mixture of the past and your hopes and aspirations.

Unbalanced vision, not enough in it for key stakeholders (customers, employees or shareholders). Vision not translated into action.	Review the vision as a team, ensuring that there is something for all the key stakeholders.
	Debate and agree plans on how the vision will be accomplished. 'A vision without a plan is a dream.' Keep pushing for actions to be completed. Be persistent – it's a key leadership responsibility.

 ## Toolkit 9 – Redoing your strategy in order to revitalise your business

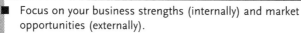

- Focus on your business strengths (internally) and market opportunities (externally).
- Significantly boost your profits.
- Create a new future for your business.

Very often businesses get locked into an existing strategy and then find it hard to change, despite the fact that their world is changing fast. One way of revitalising your business is to revisit and refine your current business strategy. Here is a checklist on redoing strategy.

1. Reduce the scope of the business

This may seem strange, but redoing your strategy normally means reducing its scope. Good strategies provide focus. For example, a building firm redefined its business in these terms: 'We were in construction but now we are in new homes development.' Success rarely comes from expanding the present scope – usually the opposite, unless of course the products and markets are in terminal free fall.

2. Have something for everyone

While making the picture as clear as possible, have something in the strategy for all the key people: customers, employees and investors. For example, decide to launch on the stock market in three years' time; allow all employees to share in the business's success; decide to build more partnerships with delighted customers.

Defining the picture in this way also enables your people to work out how to prioritise their efforts and how they can add value.

3. Exit unprofitable markets

Revitalising strategy normally means exiting unprofitable markets and culling dud products. Entrepreneurs enjoy adding products and services; they rarely kill them off. The arguments for staying in an unprofitable market need to be very strong indeed if they are to be endorsed by the review.

One house builder found that it made 8 per cent profit when it built houses for the private sector, lost 3 per cent when it built for housing associations and broke even with local authorities. The refocusing decision became easy to make.

4. Concentrate on profitable products, services and markets

It is time to go back to basics. The priorities normally followed by entrepreneurs in order of importance are:

1. Selling more to existing customers
2. Selling to new customers
3. Developing new products/services
4. Diversifying – a low priority

The principle is gardening (sell more to existing customers) rather than hunting (going looking for new opportunities). The principle of business focus is critical.

5. Develop complementary products/services

Lever existing successful products into new products. 3M levered Scotchtape into new dispensers for wrapping presents (wrist-held, like a watch), easy-to-dispense single strips and double-sided tape.

6. Involve your people

Get the people involved in the process that will be responsible for delivering the new strategy. You need buy in for the implementation stage, so get it right from the start.

The strategy review

Making strategy consists of six steps:

1. Design the new strategy.
2. Test it with the key stakeholders. Is this what the investors, managers, customers want?
3. Sell the strategy to everyone, inside the business and externally to customers and investors.

4. Cascade the strategy internally. Encourage departments to translate the strategy into their own department plans (for instance, what does the new strategy mean we should be focusing upon in the sales team?).
5. Implement the strategy. Do it. We'll have much more of this later because this is the hard part.
6. Refine it. Adapt it as the business develops.

Here's how to design the new strategy:

Step 1: Make decisions
The strategy design process consists of making a number of decisions.

> TIP: It can help to have an experienced strategic facilitator to help you work through the process. The facilitator should stick with the process and avoid getting involved with the content, by asking the questions below of the team.

In responding to the questions below, capture the answers into a strategic SWOT (strengths, weaknesses, opportunities, threats) analysis.

1. What have we learned from the past about our business that we want to retain in the future?

> ■ What are we good at – strengths/weaknesses?
> ■ What helps us compete?
> ■ What is our way of doing things that we should cherish and nurture?
> ■ Where do we make money?

2. What is happening in the world that affects us that we need to respond to?

> ■ Market trends/opportunities/threats.
> ■ Technology changes.
> ■ Competitors' activity.

3. In answering Questions 1 and 2, ask: What business should we be in, in the future?

- Re-examine scope of business.
- Focus on strengths.
- Exit from loss makers.

4. Where will we be in 3–5 years' time?

- Vision.
- Customers, investors, employees.

5. What markets specifically should we be in?

- Growth markets.
- Chance to use our strengths.
- Markets we dominate.

6. What products/services should we focus upon?

- Focus on 3–4 at most.
- Exit loss makers.

Example – CompuAdd Computer group

Q1. What have we learned from the past about our business that we want to retain in the future?

- Delivery on time is the key customer-service issue and our performance is too variable.
- Building good relationships enables us to quote for ongoing work.
- Coming from a 'box-shifting culture', we are not experienced at selling and delivering chargeable services.
- Processes are not simple and procedures don't work consistently.
- We require leading-edge product development normally reserved for large players.
- Life of products is not very long.
- Product capability, consistency and quality are the key things our customers want.
- Range of peripherals and accessories vast but wish to offer to keep control of the customer.

Q2. What is happening in our world that affects us that we need to respond to:

- Cheap imports coming from the Far East reducing prices.
- Customers want a total package and support services.
- Large competitors are targeting our traditional market segments.
- Customers want to outsource more of their computer support activities.

Q3. Where will we be in three years' time?

Shareholders:

- Our net profit before tax has increased year on year by at least 25 per cent.
- We are in a position to float or sell at a multiple-to-earnings of at least fifteen.
- We have established a business plan for our sustainable profit growth beyond flotation.
- We have chosen and focused on a target market and gained market share.

Customers:

- We have developed a set of customer-service and internal standards, which we use to measure our performance.
- We have a set of key indicators to measure our performance.
- We have refocused sales, marketing, technical and supporting functions to match the needs of customers.
- Customers recognise and value the CompuAdd difference.
- At least 80 per cent of our sales are repeat purchases (e.g., orders from retained customers).
- At least 80 per cent of our new business comes from referrals.

Employees:

- We have devolved the management of the business, creating opportunities for staff development while allowing the directors to develop the business strategically.
- We have a working environment that is conducive to teamwork and encourages initiative.
- We have an improved information system and management information system (MIS) infrastructure in place providing the tools for staff to work effectively.

- Staff who contribute share in the success of the business.
- We are seen to be one of the best employers in the area.

Q4. What markets should we be in?

- Government departments.
- IT departments or large organisations whose customers are internal departments or related organisations.

Q5. What product/service should we focus upon?

- Custom-configured PCs and servers.
- Peripherals.
- Services required for the installation and use of the above.

The strategic priorities become:

- Work with partners who can show us the way to start with.
- Simplify and automate processes so that quality procedures can be followed.
- Position company as one that uses tried/tested/stable technology.
- Internal skills to monitor marketplace for opportunities and developments.
- Stock managed efficiently (aim always to have what is required and minimise inventory).
- New products and components tested by skilled technicians prior to being offered for sale.
- Proactive approach to quality-control systems – standard configuration for manufacturing PCs (e.g., consistent slots and drivers).
- Direct delivery service from distributor to customer to reduce stockholding costs, handling and exposure to obsolescence, and to keep range broad.

The initial actions were:

- Restructure the existing board.
- Appoint Dave Osmond as operations director.
- Set up weekly cross-team meetings.
- Undertake internal management development programmes for supervisors and department heads.

In a larger more complex business it can be useful to summarise the strategic review into a strategic SWOT and then to prioritise the issues. The next example, a large Bakery was a good example.

Example – strategic SWOT analysis – 'A Bakery Limited'

Key:

First letter	H = high	Impact on the
	M = medium	business + or -
	L = low	
Second letter	H = high	Urgency to take
	M = medium	action or exploit.
	L = low	

HH should be considered for inclusion for the strategy.
Note: If no letter exists = ongoing or no action required.

STRENGTHS
Product portfolio	HH
Quality	HH
Quick to react	HH
Happy workforce and loyal	H
Innovative skills	HH
Production flexibility (plant)	H
Service levels	HH
Standing in PLC	HH

WEAKNESSES
Top team development	MH
Communication	HH
Logistics	HH
Capacity constraints	L
Forecasting sales	HH
Succession	M
Flexible working practices	HH
Training/development	HH

OPPORTUNITIES
Reputation – delicatessen	HH
Land to build	HH
Capital	MH/H
Market leadership in some sectors	M/H
Develop retail customer base	HH
Acquire businesses	M/H
Close factories	M/L
Cost reduction and efficiency	HH
Europe	LL

THREATS
Corporate inertia	HH
Input cost increases	H/M
Competitor activity	HH
Customer consolidation	MM

Legislation – working time rules (the new European directive)	H/M
Customer short-term thinking	M/H

Step 2: Now reshape

Reshape the strategy based upon the strategic SWOT (HH scores should be considered for inclusion in the new strategy).

'A' Bakery decided that their new strategy should include:

- Building a new factory and target the delicatessen sector.
- Undertaking a major cost-reduction programme.
- Installing a new briefing programme to improve communications.
- Renegotiating more flexible working practices with trade unions.
- Initiating a project to improve sales forecasting.
- Reviewing the logistics process and significantly improving.
- Selling more of their existing product portfolio using their strengths of outstanding quality and service levels in order to develop their retail customer base.

Each director and top manager was charged with the responsibility for one of the above strategic priorities.

Step 3: Sell the strategy

Find ways to sell the strategy to all the stakeholders so that everybody understands and buys into it. For instance, you might try:

- presentations by the top team to groups of staff allowing sufficient time for questions and answers
- production of a short booklet for all the staff with the new strategy
- presentations by the sales team to key customers
- a presentation by the top team of the strategy to the investors (bank or corporate HQ)

Step 4: Cascade it

Now let us take a look at the 'cascade strategy'. Cascade means encouraging departments and teams to take the overall strategy and to work out how it affects them and how they will contribute to it. For example, the strategy might call for selling our competitive advantage more effectively to retail outlets. Therefore, what's our plan to do that?

Let's look at an example of a cascade strategy to sell more to retail outlets. The sales team decide that in order to deliver the corporate strategy and sell more to retail outlets they will:

- conduct a customer survey to identify current customer perceptions
- identify core strengths and ensure they are sold by all concerned
- initiate a sales training programme to increase sales effectiveness

TIP: The cascade step is often missed, particularly for some reason in UK businesses, so the strategy floats around at the top of the business like thick cream on coffee. Don't make this mistake.

Step 5: Implementation

Now it's time to implement the new strategy. This is the tough part. Here are some of the ways successful businesses implement their strategies:

- Make someone responsible for each action point.
- Build the strategy into the annual business planning process.
- Brainstorm the blockages to delivering the strategy and remove them as a team.
- Re-establish key indicators to monitor the progress in implementing the strategy.
- Meet quarterly to review the success of your implementation plans.
- Ensure the reward system encourages people to deliver the new strategy.
- If the new strategy calls for a change in your culture then consider completing Toolkit 27, 'Creating a preferred culture'.

Troubleshooter

Potential problems

The information system is not well developed enough to be able to analyse the profitability of the products market.

Suggested remedies

Make it a top priority for the finance team to improve the costing system.

The strategy exercise is theoretical (for instance, we're spending too much time wordsmithing mission statements).	Ensure you follow the process outlined in the toolkit. Your aim is to refine your products and markets.
Managers are too busy with existing operations to implement the new strategy.	Make strategy a top management priority – no excuses. Make the resources available to free managers up to work on the strategy.

Toolkit 10 – Managing stakeholders effectively

- Ensure positive support from your key stakeholders.
- Remove blockages to progress.
- Create partnerships that advance your strategy.

Stakeholders are those people who can affect or are affected by your business activities, including family, investors, customers, key employees, government agencies and potentially many others.

Successful strategies require good analysis (being smart) but their implementation also calls for political skills (being wise). This means getting buy-in to the strategy and its consequences from the people it affects or can affect it (the stakeholders).

Too often good plans are unable to be rolled out because a key stakeholder is not on board. For instance, the bank won't increase their lending, a colleague on the management team does not support the plan, a key customer changes their trading terms, or a supplier significantly increases their prices without any prior warning. The leadership task is to:

- Identify all key stakeholders.
- Determine their current position with regard to your business plans – are they supporters or opponents?
- Do the 'political work' in order to get your key stakeholders to buy into your plans.

Step 1: Make a list
List all the people who can affect or are affected by your business plans.

	Step 1	Step 2	Step 3
	Names	Rating 1–10	+ - =
Family members			
Key customers			
Suppliers			
Key staff			
Colleagues			
Add your own			
stakeholders to			
this list:			

Step 2: Rating your stakeholders

Now rate the importance of each stakeholder out of 10. 1 = low, 10 = a key stakeholder. Ask yourself: 'Who could really help me to deliver the plan/get the job done? Who could seriously make it very difficult to implement the plan/get the job done?'

Use the scale 1–10 to assess their relative importance.

Step 3: Reviewing your stakeholders

Review your stakeholders' current positions in terms of their current commitment to your business or plans. Try to classify them into: allies (+), adversaries (-), fence sitters (=)

Allies are people who will or are currently supporting your business. There are a number of indicators that stakeholders may be allies:

- They have supported you in the past.
- You have a positive relationship with them.
- They are already committed to supporting you in actions, not just words.
- You are able to do things for them (win–win).

Adversaries actively oppose your business plan. Indicators that stakeholders may be adversaries include:

- Not supported you in the past (when they could have).
- No relationship exists.
- They have stated that they will not support you.
- You are unable to do anything for them.

Fence sitters are difficult to assess because at this stage they neither support nor oppose you. Indicators of fence sitters are:

- They say they may support you but as yet have not taken any action.
- You have not yet had an opportunity to find out.
- They may be in a difficult political position – should they support or oppose you?
- There are no consequences for them, either positive or negative, for supporting you.

Clearly, to be able to complete Step 3 you need to be able to make a considered assessment of the stance your stakeholders might take to your plans.

You may need to have a dialogue with them at the appropriate time in order to assess their position.

Example

Stakeholder analysis – a leisure business					
Stakeholder	Rating	+	-	=	Notes
Father	5			✔	Taking a back seat
Brother	8	✔			V. positive to plan
Sales manager	9		✔		Felt threatened
Service manager	8		✔		Opposed the plan
Bank	7			✔	
Accountant	3			✔	

Story – The Two American Presidents

One American president was regarded as not the smartest (he hadn't been to Harvard) but he was very politically astute (i.e. wise). The other was very smart (Harvard and Oxford) but when he took office he was politically naïve.

The first president wanted to initiate the 'Star Wars' initiative. So before he was elected he visited key senators (stakeholders) and identified his allies, adversaries and fence sitters. He found out their interests and promised to help them once he got into office. Once elected he announced his Star Wars plan and got it through the House without a problem.

The second president announced he was going to improve healthcare and put his wife in charge of the project. They developed a plan without contacting too many senators. Once elected, the president presented his new healthcare plan and most senators voted against it.

Moral: If you don't do the political work and manage your stakeholders well, then the smartest plan in the world may well be opposed.

Step 4: Encourage allies

Determine what needs to be done to encourage allies to champion your plans for you, deal effectively with adversaries or neutralise their potential negative impact and get fence sitters *off* the fence.

Example – Getting buy-in

Strategies to get buy-in from stakeholders that have worked include:

- Making a presentation to them in order to sell your ideas and to get them on board (tip: be enthusiastic at your presentation – enthusiasm is infectious).
- Listening very carefully to their views.
- Simply asking for their help.
- Identifying what they want and delivering it for them.
- Negotiating a win–win position with them.
- Finding out whom they respect and getting those people to influence your stakeholders (third party).
- Inviting them to help you deliver your strategy.
- Getting your allies (+) to help you sell your plans to other stakeholders.
- Being persistent in getting their buy-in – don't take no for an answer.
- Making sure you keep them informed of progress (for instance, banks often assume no news is bad news).
- Finally, seeking to neutralise their impact if they won't play ball.

Step 5: A stakeholder plan

Make a stakeholder plan and stick to it. See it as a key role for senior managers to keep key stakeholders on side.

Example – stakeholder plan for a leisure business

- Get brother to work on sales manager (his friend and fellow football fan) to build his commitment to the plan.

- MD to identify service manager's needs in order to fulfil them and then get him to support the plan.

- Use Toolkit 28, 'Fixing system slippage', to raise funds to reduce overdraft and get bank support.

- Invite accountant to spend more time in the business to get them to support the business more actively.

Troubleshooter

Potential problems	Suggested remedies
Adversary proves difficult to manage.	Find someone your adversary trusts and values and ask them to help you. Try talking directly, honestly and passionately to them – this often works.
Hard to get people off the fence to support you actively.	Try to find out what their interests might be and do something for them. Then they might support you.
You don't have the necessary 'political skills'.	Find someone in your business who does and get them to help you.

CHAPTER FOUR

Developing Your Team

Toolkits 11–15

Toolkit 11: Picking the right people
Toolkit 12: Clarify the key roles in your business
Toolkit 13: How to achieve your business goals by really motivating your top team
Toolkit 14: Dealing with supervisory slippage
Toolkit 15: Let go to grow

Toolkit 11: Picking the right people

- Avoid expensive mistakes and, even worse, mediocrity.
- Reduce turnover in your team.
- Create a team that enjoys working together.

A recent London Business School survey of CEOs showed that the major factor that contributes to the success of their businesses was 'selecting the right people with good attitudes who are loyal to the company and who want to excel in their careers'.

It has long been recognised that the two key tasks of a CEO are developing a winning strategy (see Toolkit 9 'Redoing your strategy in order to revitalise your business') and picking the people capable of delivering the strategy.

This toolkit was written to help with the vital task of picking the right people in your business.

Story – CompuAdd Computer Group

'We had been through three CEOs before we found Dave Osmond,' says Martin Vincent, chairman of CompuAdd. 'We worked through the "Redoing your strategy" toolkit [Toolkit 9] and developed what we all believed to be a winning strategy. Unfortunately, we did not have the top team at that time capable of delivering the strategy. We reorganised the board and unfortunately two directors had to go. We were struggling along until I appointed Dave Osmond. Then the business took off. Picking the right people has been a real lesson for us over the past five years.'

My personal experience has been that the difference between somebody who is just OK for the job and somebody who excels is not a percentage point at the margin: it's usually incalculable.

Here's how to develop your team:

Step 1: Write a description
Draw a description of the job you need doing. Update the job guide/description, as circumstances will almost certainly have changed since you recruited for the role.

Ask what are our strategic priorities right now. Write them down. Looking at the balance of your existing team, which tasks or priorities are not currently covered.

For example, if customers are leaving and no one is finding out why, then the business has a problem. What gaps or duplications do you have in your existing processes or output?

Draw up a description of the job you need doing.

> TIP: Make sure you really do think clearly about what the business needs.

Step 2: Write a profile
Draw up the profile of the person you wish to recruit. There are hundreds of books on recruitment and selection that cover writing job guides and personnel specs in great detail, so I don't intend to repeat that knowledge. However, in selecting people for top jobs, it is often helpful to ask what are the key skills and attributes that someone would need to be able to do the job outlined in step. List them.

Step 3: The candidates

Create some candidates. For top jobs the major sources of candidates are (and note that the relative cost and difficulties increase from the first to the last):

- internal candidates
- people we know in the industry whom we can approach
- advertising (remember: even a recruitment advert can provide a positive or negative image of your business; for instance, a restaurant placed an expensive large advert in a Sheffield newspaper for a lavish Christmas dinner, but on the opposite page they also placed a large advert for a head chef, head waiter and other restaurant staff!)
- headhunting

TIPS:

- Your ability to find a suitable internal candidate is the acid test of your succession planning system. If you lack strong internal candidates, this might be a time to review that process.
- Consider offering business incentives to existing employees for providing leads for successful appointments.
- Headhunting is expensive but you generally pay only for the result.

Step 4: The selection process

Now comes the time for setting up the selection process. Draw up an interview list, but be ruthless – time is precious (yours and theirs).

Use the criteria previously established.

TIP: Keep records of candidates and decision criteria, because increasingly rejected candidates sue for unfair selection. And treat every candidate as a potential customer. If they don't get the job they might end up with a competitor or as a customer of yours.

When inviting people for interviews tell them what the steps in the process will be and how long it will take. Ask yourself how you will know or assess whether the candidate has the attributes.

TIP: Highlight a maximum of four or five critical attributes.

Alternatives to interviews

Ask candidates to make a presentation on how they would approach the job. This tests how they think, their presentation skills, knowledge of the area and commitment.

Consider psychometric tests. Use a registered tester. You can test for skills and personality. If social skills are important consider setting up a meeting with their peer team in your business.

> TIP: Write down your criteria, the questions and space to record the answers. People get sidetracked in interviews and they don't stay focused. Writing down your plan really helps.

Step 5: The interview

Now we come to the interview itself. There are two options for interviews:

> ■ A general screening to reduce to a short list. This may be undertaken by one person.
>
> ■ Straight into the main interview. It is suggested that two people carry out this process: the individual's direct boss and one other appropriate person.

Ask yourself what evidence will be required to convince you that the candidate has the skills and experience you are looking for. For example, if the role demanded selling to a retailer, then one of the attributes you would look for is sales planning. Go for specific believable examples to confirm experiences against your criteria. For instance:

YOU: 'Give me an example of a time when you made a significant improvement to sales in your business.'

CANDIDATE: 'Over the last year I increased sales by 3 per cent.'

YOU: 'What I am after is a specific example of what you did. Describe exactly how you went about it?'

> TIP: Look for candidate saying I or 'we': that may mean they have not personally done it.

Carry on probing to satisfy yourself that the candidate has the experience and attributes you require:

YOU: How did you increase sales?

CANDIDATE: I worked more effectively …

YOU: But what did you actually do?

If they cannot answer they have probably not had the experience. Keep going until you are convinced they have what you need to do the job (or not).

> TIP: Most interviewers spend 90 per cent of the time on the biography of the candidate. Avoid this unless the candidate's school, hobbies and family are critical for success! Focus on the criteria that are critical to the job and save everybody's time.

Compare each candidate to the criteria, not against each other. By the end of the selection interviews if you stuck with focusing upon your required criteria the choice should be obvious. If you are not sure, is it because you have several good candidates or that none of them meets the criteria? If it's the latter, don't appoint: start again.

If you have more than one good candidate, consider the risks that would be involved in the appointment of each candidate, and then select the one who provides the least risk.

As soon as you have made your decision, let the successful candidate know quickly.

> TIP: In order to create a positive response to your offer, tell candidates you will inform them of the outcome within one week and then call them the next day. For added candidate delight, ring them the night of the interview.

> TIP: It's your business, the final decision comes down to: Can you see yourself working with the candidate for the next five years? Do you personally like them? If so, go ahead; if not, think again.

Troubleshooter

Potential problems	Suggested remedies
Can't get good people to apply.	Consider offering incentives to existing staff to bring candidates. Consider headhunting the best people available.

The halo effect: you pick people in your image.	Stick to the criteria you established. Get someone else to interview candidates as well as you.
We need somebody, therefore we appoint somebody who is not quite right for the job.	Do a risk analysis before you appoint. Try reorganising internally to avoid having to make a poor appointment.
Appoint the wrong person.	Seek legal advice and get rid of them as quickly and as cheaply as possible.

Toolkit 12: Clarify the key roles in your business

- Ensure your key resources are focused on the right priorities for your business.
- Help your people to add value and not cost.
- Ensure the successful delivery of your strategic priorities.

People do one of two things in business: they either add value or they add cost – there are no grey areas. One of the ways that you can ensure that your senior team are adding value is to help them to clarify their roles.

Role clarification

There are a number of fairly common problems that point to a need for role clarification.

Role ambiguity

This arises where there is uncertainty in the mind of the jobholder or others in your organisation as to what their and your roles are. Their confusion throws up questions such as:

- How can I add real value right now to our business?
- How much emphasis should I put on strategy or operations?
- For what areas of work can I take initiatives?
- What are the strategic priorities, because the strategy is unclear?

Role conflict

Role conflict can occur where the jobholder has to carry out more than one role in the same situation. She/he can experience tensions.

For instance, a manager may be torn in loyalty between supporting the performance or actions of his/her own staff and acting as the representative of senior managers.

Role overload
This arises where the number of different roles that a person is asked to perform is excessive. This is different from overwork – although often involves this as well.

Role underload
Role underload occurs where a person feels she/he has the capacity to handle a more complex or a wider set of roles.

Role clarification – the background

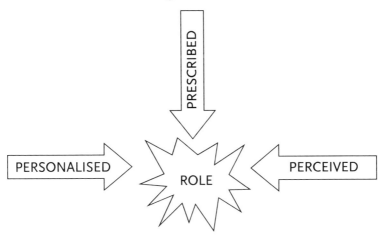

Prescribed role
The prescribed role is what the organisation uses to set down people's expected contributions to the overall goals and objectives. It is normally defined in a 'job description', which sets out responsibilities, authority, key tasks and location in the organisational hierarchy.

This is a mechanistic view of role, which does not take account of personal differences and changes of circumstances such as growth of the business and need to cover weaknesses in performance of others.

Personalised role
The prescribed role is only part of the picture. There are factors internal to the individual, which will affect the way she/he performs the role:

Abilities, skills, professional competence, strengths

Expectations	'I see this job as a stepping stone to ...'
Values	'In my view employee relations are about ...'
Assumptions	'My manager is really interested in ...'
Qualities	Assertiveness, patience
Uncertainty	'I'm not sure that I can ...'
Vision	'I want to achieve ...'

Perceived role

The perceptions and expectations of others in the organisation will affect the prescribed role and the personalised role. Others will have views on what the priorities for the job should be ('I don't want contract managers getting involved in ...').

Others will have apprehensions, expectations and doubts about the way in which the job should be carried out. As the jobholder interacts with these people, their perception will constrain and limit their behaviour.

Role clarification – A solution

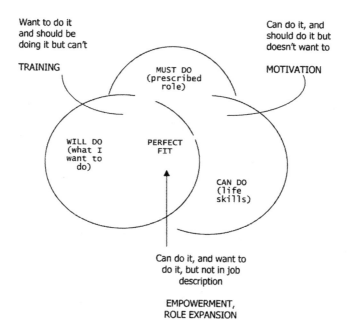

Want to do it
and should be
doing it but can't

TRAINING

Can do it, and
should do it but
doesn't want to

MOTIVATION

MUST DO
(prescribed role)

WILL DO
(what I
want to
do)

PERFECT
FIT

CAN DO
(life
skills)

Can do it, and want to
do it, but not in job
description

EMPOWERMENT,
ROLE EXPANSION

How to do it

> TIP: It is sometimes helpful to use a skilled facilitator to undertake this process.

Step 1

> TIP: Don't ask them to get their job description out of the drawer. It's almost certain they never read it.

Ask the role holder to describe their role as they see it. Push for them to describe what they actually do:

- 'I go out and win new business.'
- 'I keep a close eye on the key indicators.'
- 'I see my role as motivating the team to really perform.'

Ask them what they see the business priorities to be right now and their role in delivering it. Ask them what they must do, like doing or choose to do?

Step 2

Ask the role holder how they see their boss undertaking the role. Ask them to be honest and to look at the role and not the personality.

- What do they focus upon?
- What parts of the role are being ignored?
- What should they do more of?

> TIP: Allow people space to talk. Deliberately leave gaps in the discussion to allow them to fill them. Try to say as little as possible.

Step 3

Ask their boss for their views on the role (not the personality); in other words, what they do rather than who they are.

- What do they see as the strategic priorities?
- What does the role holder do really well?
- What parts of the role get neglected?
- What could the role holder do more of?

Step 4

Summarise the feedback from the questions posed in Steps 1–3 into bullet points. Discuss the overall views of the role holder, their team and their boss.

> ■ Are there any themes emerging (e.g., all say the role holder is an excellent communicator)?
>
> ■ Are there any significant differences between the views? If so, why?
>
> ■ What does the role holder take from it?

Here is a live example of Steps 1–3 together with the action plan that was developed as a result of Step 4.

BJ: role clarification

BJ was a MD of a division of a large construction group in the west of England. He came from a project-management background and enjoyed rolling up his sleeves and project-managing. There was a feeling he was not fulfilling the strategic role of the MD. He felt he was doing a good job and was reluctant to change.

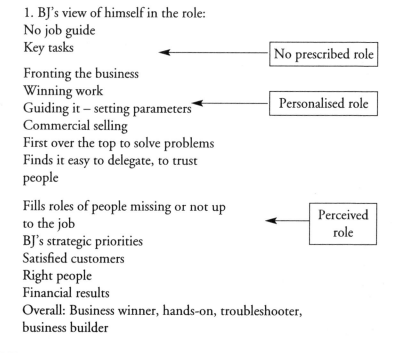

1. BJ's view of himself in the role:
No job guide
Key tasks ← No prescribed role

Fronting the business
Winning work
Guiding it – setting parameters ← Personalised role
Commercial selling
First over the top to solve problems
Finds it easy to delegate, to trust
people

Fills roles of people missing or not up
to the job ← Perceived role
BJ's strategic priorities
Satisfied customers
Right people
Financial results
Overall: Business winner, hands-on, troubleshooter,
business builder

2. BJ's team view of BJ:

Close team, very flexible

Strong charismatic, leadership style (can sometimes cause a halo effect: i.e., everything that BJ does is good)

Areas they thought BJ should consider developing:

More networking with longer-term partners

Need a clearer strategy

Need to backfill systems – IT etc.

Need to free up time to work *on* as well as *in* the business

Need to take training and development of staff much more seriously

Develop teams to enable directors to direct and not be so 'hands-on' operational

Need to improve internal communications

3. BJ's bosses' view of BJ:

Good role model

Very hardworking, hands-on

Very good project-management skills

Areas to consider developing:

Use of systems to control business more effectively

Networking with targeted partners – longer-term

Focus on priorities (not necessarily immediate problems)

Being open-minded and listening

Taking more responsibility for reportage

Do 'system slippage' investigations

Need to turn strategic priorities into objectives for people (for example, more focused delegation)

BJ's review – action plan

- Get a clear strategy.
- Spend more time networking.
- Create time to direct and work on, as well as in, the business.
- Improve systems.
- Develop a training plan.
- Improve internal communications.

BJ really benefited from the role clarification that came from his boss and his team. It helped him to consider his prescribed role as

MD and that the role demanded more than just following his project-management inclinations (personalised role). He responded positively to the feedback.

Step 5

Repeat the exercise with all members of the team. This enables the CEO to be certain that the top team are focusing their energies on the strategic priorities of the business. It also significantly increases the chances of long-term success.

Toolkit 13: How to achieve your business goals by really motivating your top team

> ■ Ensure your top team is individually motivated.
> ■ Align business aims with the top team's individual rewards.
> ■ Create a common purpose in your top team.

The recipe for success has been well established:

1. Set clear objectives
2. Make sure your reward system is aligned to the achievement of the objectives

If you want to improve your business performance or change your culture, then ensure the reward system supports the process.

Story – Northwest.com

> A b-to-b dotcom based in Manchester was looking for fast growth. The CEO decided to try to align individual commitment in her top team with the requirements of the business.
>
> 'I got the guys together and asked them what they wanted individually; initially they were somewhat surprised and suspicious,' she says.
>
> 'I persisted and, once one came clean that he wanted a bonus amounting to 50 per cent of his salary, the rest jumped in. One wanted two months' paid leave to take a holiday in Australia, one wanted a Subaru Imprezza car – no accounting for taste!
>
> 'I had decided and agreed with our investors that we were looking for a growth from £1.5 million to £10 million in sales and £1.5 million net profits in the next eighteen months.

'We agreed to meet their individual incentives, provided we hit business targets. The change in their behaviour was remarkable. They immediately started collaborating much more effectively, egos went out of the window and they started operating as a real team for the first time. "Me" changed to "we" overnight. The buzz and commitment was infectious. They beat the business target and deserved to enjoy their personal rewards.'

Step 1: Assemble the team

Get your top team together and ask them individually what they really want personally. Is it a big car? A share in the business? A holiday in Hawaii? More time with their family? Whatever it is, make a note of what they say.

Examples

Let's look at three examples …

A technical IT person in Perth, Australia, wanted to work half time for two years when his son was born. The company agreed and felt they got as much out of him as they needed, if not much more. At the same time the business doubled in size in line with their goals.

A sales director in an advertising agency in London wanted an Aston Martin. The CEO agreed that if he brought in three new targeted accounts then he could have one. He did and they gave him one.

American companies are much more likely than British counterparts to give away equity. They figure it ties their top talent into the business. This might explain why they often enjoy much faster growth rates than their British equivalents.

Step 2: Do the sums

Calculate the cost of the things people say they want in total. For instance, 'It comes to an additional cost of £100k to the business.'

Step 3: Do the deal

Tell your team they can all have what they want provided you get what your business needs in order to provide it for them.

This is likely to be more than the £100k additional cost. For instance, you might say, 'We want sales to increase by 50 per cent, not 20 per cent, and profits up by 100 per cent, not 30 per cent.'

> TIP: Make the business targets worth achieving.

Step 4: Forging a common purpose

Get your top team to recognise that in order for them to get their rewards as individuals they will need to work together – to forge a common purpose.

Get them to commit to the common purpose (the business objectives) and to work out how they intend to collaborate in order to achieve the common purpose.

This will probably involve removing blockages between them, collaborating, suspending egos and turf wars, sharing resources and talking to each other regularly and often.

You want them to form a strong team: $1+1+1+1 = 10$ – the synergy you get when people really do collaborate and work together towards a common purpose.

Step 5: Now go higher

Celebrate success and reset bigger targets!

Summary

This is potentially a very powerful process, but it needs handling properly. Consider getting advice and support to help you to undertake it well.

Toolkit 14: Dealing with supervisory slippage

> ■ Set and maintain high standards.
> ■ Help your managers and supervisors to do their job effectively.
> ■ Ensure tasks get completed.

This is a short, simple but potentially very powerful and important toolkit. Most businesses get things done through people. Supervising people and processes are therefore the key tasks needed to get the work of the business completed successfully.

However, in some businesses you hear the following complaints:

- 'We start lots of initiatives but never seem to get many completed.'
- 'We seem to be always juggling lots of balls at once here.'
- 'We keep making the same mistakes.'
- 'We often produce results beneath rather than beyond expectations.'
- 'We seem to have problems in maintaining standards at the sharp end.'
- 'We have a plan but we can't make it work.'

These could be indicators of a common business problem: supervisory slippage.

Story – Fred Buijs, Nestlé, East London, South Africa

Fred the factory manager has developed his own unique way of preventing supervisory slippage. He gets a daily briefing from his manager about what's happening in the factory that day. He then undertakes some 'management by walking around' (MBWA).

When he meets a supervisor he asks how things are going and how they would personally assess their own progress. He pulls out three cards from his pocket: red, yellow and green. Red is 'bad performance or slippage', yellow is 'just OK' and green is 'on track, no slippage'. He asks the supervisors to pick a colour (review themselves) and then they agree to improve ('Green next time I come around'). This creates a bit of banter and a laugh but it does have a real impact on preventing supervisory slippage in his factory.

The key point was that Fred was constantly getting people to think about their job, review progress and take actions to improve.

Here is how it happens in practice:

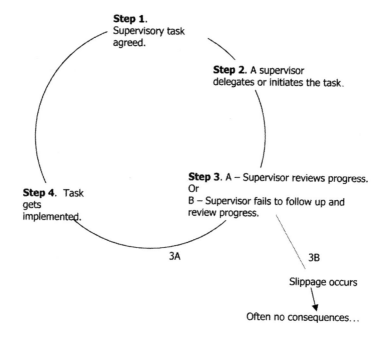

Step 1: Agreeing the task

The supervisory task is agreed with the supervisor. This can be to take a decision, solve a problem, initiate improvements or just ensure the job gets done to the agreed standards.

For example, ensure all deliveries are dispatched on time or make sure the department responds to all customer queries the same day.

Step 2: Delegating the task

The supervisor delegates the task to individuals or a team, explaining to them what's required, by when and to what standard: 'We need to make sure all deliveries are dispatched on time and that we record the details accurately on the dispatch record. Any questions, team? I'll check with you every two hours to see how you're doing.'

Step 3: Watching for slippage

The supervisor checks every two hours to ensure deliveries go on time, or the supervisor is 'too busy' on other jobs and forgets to monitor the task. Consequently slippage may occur and the job does not get done.

The crucial step is Step 3 – the review of progress. How are we doing?

If a supervisor is too busy to follow up and complete the review there is a chance that the task will slip (see diagram: 3B).

The problem is that this also creates a culture that says to people, 'Don't bother seeing things through: nobody really cares'; or 'Here we go again, another initiative; if we keep our heads down it'll go away.'

A culture of complacency and not finishing things off is a dangerous one to encourage, even by default.

Story – Brian Crawshaw, Bramall Construction

Brian Crawshaw, the production director of Bramall Construction in South Yorkshire, understands the problems system slippage can create.

'We run up to twenty construction sites across the North of England. We employ really good guys on site, but we can incur such high penalties for not completing projects on time that ensuring slippages do not occur is a key part of my job.

'I agree actions with my supervisors and record them in a notebook. I am constantly going around asking, "How are we doing with so and so? Did we get that delivery as promised?" I follow everything up.

'I try to do it in a helpful, encouraging way. I think we now have a culture where very little slippage occurs. The results are that we finish all our jobs within the agreed deadlines and our customers are delighted with us.'

This is hard graft day in day out. You don't need an MBA to do it, but Brian's work almost certainly provides Bramall's with its competitive edge, and that's the point.

Here are some actions to take to create a culture of positive supervision that produces results and gets the job done:

- Train your supervisors in the 'plan – do – review' cycle.
- Make it part of people's roles.
- Get into the habit of telling people at all levels, 'Update me on what's happening about X task.' Be like Brian Crawshaw!

- Be a role model for reviewing progress.
- Act like Fred Buijs in the Nestlé story.
- Build review into your management meetings.
- Make it part of your culture.
- Hold people responsible for achieving agreed deadlines – whatever it takes.

TIP: Publish a list of initiatives/projects with names, objectives and outcomes to everybody in the business. One engineering company found it had over five hundred different initiatives, many of them duplicating others, which few people knew about. These projects were consuming over 30 per cent of the management and supervisory time. Few were ever completed successfully.

If a serious slippage does occur hold a full postmortem and build the lessons into your business process.

Toolkit 15: Let go to grow

- Delegate successfully in order to grow your business and yourself.
- Create a team-managed business.
- Remove any major obstacles to growth.

One of the biggest challenges that growing businesses face is moving from owner- or CEO-managed to team-managed. This allows the owner/CEO to focus externally on longer-term issues rather than day-to-day performance.

A study by London Business School revealed that 84 per cent of growth businesses had found that the capacity of the management team was the biggest internal barrier to growth.

Why? Maybe because individuals responsible for the business face many demands on their time and energy and the need to work on several things at once, while being consumed by the day-to-day and obsessed about the future, and confronting the reality that they can work only through other people.

Many of the traditional business remedies to this problem don't really work very well. I know because I have tried most of them:

- Attending a time-management course.
- Attending a team-building workshop.
- Trying to 'delegate' to people.

When top managers do try to let go, they either can't, so they fiddle and annoy people, or they abdicate. Neither approach is very effective. You are going to be smarter than that ...

Story – A Personal Experience

In 1995 I was running a £5 million consultancy business from fourteen offices across the UK. We had started off on the dining table in 1987 and by 1995 employed a hundred people.

As my role changed from doing everything to being chairman, I realised that I had to let go and delegate more to my team. I found this hard, so I went on a time-management course about setting objectives, prioritising and delegating. I understood the theory at an intellectual level about my need to delegate, but like many owner-managers I found it impossible to do in practice. I was the business and the business was me. I couldn't give up doing the things I enjoyed and I thought was pretty good at.

My team were getting increasingly frustrated at my apparent unwillingness to trust them, delegate and let go.

Then one day my doctor told me I could work only one day a week for three months. This was an instruction, not a suggestion!

For the first time in my life I had to ask myself: What is it I do that my team can do? What is it only I can do? What is it I do that nobody should be doing? (There was quite a lot of that!)

I was forced to let go and delegate – no choice. This was a watershed in my business because once I let go I realised that I didn't want to run the business. I had been too busy being busy that I failed to recognise the fact that I was bored with the business and wanted out.

I sold my business to my team for a healthy profit and moved on. This was the best decision I ever made, because I love what I do now.

The point of this story is not to recommend that you sell up but to illustrate how it took an illness to make me let go and delegate and how difficult that process is for entrepreneurs.

What can you learn from this story? If you are struggling to let go and delegate to your team, imagine you can work only one day a week and ask yourself the questions we saw above:

- I have a day a week – what is it that only I must do in my business?
- What is it that I do that my team could do?
- What do I do that nobody should do?

Be tough in answering these questions. Maybe ask your partner, wife or husband to help.

Story – CompuAdd Computers

'When I was promoted to the role of managing director from sales director I really found it difficult to let go and allow my managers to manage,' says Dave Osmond.

'I loved sales, so I could not stop myself from getting involved in the details of sales. My team suggested I attend a workshop on time planning. The principles were obvious: set your objectives, then plan your time. Intellectually I understood it but emotionally I could not let go of sales. I realised that perhaps deep down I didn't trust the sales team; I felt I needed to be involved in the detail.

'Then one day I discovered the "let go to grow" process and put it into practice. It worked like a dream for me. I am now focusing on the key tasks of the MD and the whole business has benefited.'

This is a time-tested way of dealing with the emotional issue of letting go, delegating and sleeping easy in your bed.

Step 1: Clarifying your role
Clarify your role in the business for the future. What should be your priorities?

Try using the prioritising method. For instance, you could say, 'Our strategy/plans/priorities call for.................................... Therefore, I should be focusing upon.................................'

If you are the leader then your key leadership tasks include:

- Setting the strategy.
- Picking the people capable of delivering the strategy.
- Spending time building the business for the future, perhaps as much as 50 per cent outside the business with customers and stakeholders.
- Encouraging working ON your business.

Example

Tom Hunter of Sports Division enjoyed being the team leader and he was the best buyer in his business. He decided to focus on these roles and dropped other things.

Step 2: Delegating

Once you have decided your role priorities using Toolkit 12, 'Clarify the key roles in your business', consider what aspects of it you intend to delegate to others. Consider who is really capable and ready for development. Who are the people for the future?

Pick people with energy and commitment who will relish the challenge.

TIP: Try picking some young people. You don't have to be 64 to manage projects or companies!

Step 3: Agree objectives

Tell the people you have selected to delegate to that you intend to focus on some key areas and you intend to delegate part of your role to them personally. Say you believe they are ready to take on a bigger role and give them the responsibility and accountability to undertake the new tasks.

Agree the objectives with them in detail (the *what*). These might be: 'To look after the distribution of our products and improve the delivery performance from 65–95 per cent on time over the next six months' or 'To launch three new products by the end of 2002 as part of our agreed business development process'.

Step 4: An action plan

Ask the individuals to produce a one-page action plan of the steps they intend to take to achieve the objectives (the *how*). This plan (a sort of mental rehearsal) lets them do the thinking. This develops them and gives them ownership of the task (see the action plan in Toolkit 5, 'Providing leadership'). It also allows you to check their thinking and plans before taking any action.

You can then either sign off the plan or coach them in any areas for improvement. Either way, you sleep easy in your bed because they own the task and the job gets done.

Step 5: Talk to the team

Make sure you spend enough time with your people, passing on your wisdom about the way you want your business to be run. This is particularly important when you are moving from an owner-managed to a team-managed business.

Remember, you know how to do things, because you have probably spent years working at it. However, the tasks may well be new to your people, and you have to invest time in passing on your experience. So delegate and coach. Don't abdicate and hope…

> TIP: Don't fall into the bureaucratic trap of trying to record everything you do in a systems manual. You need to build the business by building your culture (see Toolkit 27, 'Creating a preferred culture').

Step 6: Assessing progress

Continue to show interest in their work. Use the action plans to assess progress. Congratulate them publicly on their successes.

Step 7: Focus

Focus on your new role without falling into the trap of either getting overinvolved in the delegated task or abdicating and then worrying about what's happening.

> TIP: Learn to master the three Ds – do it, diary it or dump it – and you will create time for the really important tasks you need to complete.

Summary

If you let go well, then you will create time to focus on the important aspects of your role.

CHAPTER FIVE

Customerising: Getting Much Closer to Your Customers

Toolkits 16–19

Toolkit 16: Conducting a customer perception survey
Toolkit 17: Removing the obstacles your customers face
buying from you
Toolkit 18: Getting customer service right
Toolkit 19: Build your business by delighting customers

Toolkit 16: Conducting a customer perception survey

- Review your business through your customers' eyes.
- Prioritise issues for improvement.
- Gain competitive advantage by giving your customers what they really want.

Successful businesses take the pulse of how well they are performing by conducting regular customer perception surveys. Standing in the customers' shoes in order to provide objective feedback is the way to ensure that you keep up with customers' expectations and ahead of your competitors.

Customer perception surveys also prevent businesses becoming complacent and even arrogant, sometimes eventually losing the plot.

There are many benefits to conducting a customer survey. A survey

- Tells you what your customers want.
- Provides feedback on how they see you.
- Highlights areas for improvement.
- Shows customers you care about their opinions.
- Helps you listen to your customers.
- Keeps you abreast of competitors' strengths and weaknesses.
- Provides the basis for a business plan based on objective evidence.
- Provides sales people with ammunition to sell your business.

Story – North East Engineering Inc.

'We must be OK with customers because we don't get many complaints,' said the CEO of North East Engineering Inc. in 1995.

He was persuaded to find out the facts. A customer attitude survey, with a random sample of 100 customers in each of his key market segments, was conducted by telephone. The main survey revealed:

Priority of purchase	Rating	Competitors' rating
1. Price	6	6
2. Delivery	2	8
3. Sales and service support	3	8
4. Technical support	5	5

Clearly the priority was to improve delivery and sales and service support.

He acted immediately and set up a project to identify ways of improving delivery performance. This became a major project that resulted in a significant improvement in deliveries on time from 60 to 95 per cent.

The sales-and-service support team were trained in customer care and service; new standards were established.

This also resulted in a significant boost to the service performance. 'In a difficult market we need to do all we can to stay attractive to customers and to beat the competition,' he says.

'A follow-up survey in 1999 demonstrated that the service ratings had been maintained, and that is good news.'

Customer surveys produce invaluable data but this story demonstrates it's what you do with the information that is important.

Step 1: Which survey?

Decide your preferred method of survey to your customers. Here are the pros and cons of the different methods.

A postal survey

Advantages	Disadvantages
Cheap	Often a very limited response level –
Does not take much time	e.g., 5 per cent
Possible to survey large	Bias due to type of people responding
number of customers	Impossible to gauge levels of feeling or
	probe for more information

Face-to-face survey

Advantages	Disadvantages
Allows for probing questions	Very time-consuming
More detailed answers	Can be very expensive
Increases customer contact	

Telephone survey

Advantages	Disadvantages
Good for b-to-b	Consumers fed up with telephone
Allows for probing	survey.
Larger response than post	More time consuming and more
Detailed perceptions can be	expensive than post
obtained	
Can provide reasonably deep	
insights into customer perception	

Pick the survey method you believe is best suited to your business.

Step 2: Decide who will conduct it

Determine who is best suited to conduct the survey. There are two options: your own staff and a third party.

Self or own staff

Advantages	Disadvantages
Good knowledge of the business	Inexperienced in conducting surveys
Can sort facts from opinions	Customers may think you are selling
Cheaper	May be biased

Consultants or other third party

Advantages	Disadvantages
Objective, no axe to grind	Unfamiliar with the nuances of your business
	More expensive

Step 3: Decide on customers

Decide which customers you want to contact. You need to survey a broad cross-section of customers in terms of:

- The size of their business.
- Volume of business they do with you.
- Type of business.
- Geographic location.
- Length of time they have been customers (include both old and new).
- Ex-customers (you need to know why they went somewhere else).
- People who asked you to quote but who did not choose to buy from you.

If you have a customer base of up to 500 names, you should aim to survey 30–50 responses. If your customer base numbers more than 500, then I suggest 80–100 organisations should be involved in the survey.

If time or resources are limited, then I suggest you talk to your major customers, for example the top 20 per cent and/or the 'hottest' prospects for the future.

The selection of which customers to contact should be made randomly to prevent people picking their favourites, which gives bias to the results. Random sampling also allows you to examine a much smaller number of customers and still have confidence in the results.

You need to think about which people in your customers' business you want to talk to, be it buyers, accountants or the MD.

It can be helpful to review the decision-making unit in your customers. Who actually makes the decisions? Who is the MAN (the person with the *M*oney, *A*uthority, *N*eed)? These are often different people.

Make sure you survey the right people in the decision-making unit in your customers. As a guide, in businesses of up to 500 employees there can be up to three people involved in the process, but, in those with more than 1,000 employees, more than six people can get involved in influencing buying decisions.

Before starting the survey, check all your customer details to make sure that they are up to date. This will also highlight any deficiencies in your customer records system. (A newspaper business found that 20 per cent of their customer list was out of date. They even called up three customers who had been dead a year!)

Step 4: Design the questionnaire

Design and pilot the questionnaire. It should be short, no more than ten questions, and should not take your customer more than 10–15 minutes to complete.

I once received a 284-part postal questionnaire from BMW, which I reckon would have taken me over an hour to complete. Guess what I did with it …

Create one questionnaire per customer with a space at the top to record their name, organisation, date and the name of the interviewee.

Type the questions and leave a space for the interviewee to record the customer comments verbatim. They must be instructed to write down exactly what the customer says and not reinterpret. For instance, if the customer says, 'I think you are OK on deliveries', the interviewer should not write, 'Customer very satisfied with the delivery performance'.

Here are the primary customer perception questions to ask:

Q1. What do you look for in a supplier?
Probe:
If they say one or two things ask
what else until you get their full list.
Check by asking, 'Is that everything?' $\longrightarrow$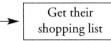

Q2. Which of these factors in Q1 is most important to you?

Put them in order (say, 1–5). ────────→ | Prioritise their shopping list |

Q3. On a scale of 1–10 (1 = awful, 10 = perfect), how do we rate on the factors in Q2?
Don't disagree with them, just record their observations. ────────→ | How they rate you on their prioritised shopping list |

Q4. How do our competitors rate on the same scale?
They will not always give you this information. ────────→ | Competitive benchmarking |
If you are doing well, ask them for the names of who they see as your main competitors.

There are some additional questions you can ask, but if you get Questions 1–4 in detail you probably have most of what you need already.

Here are some additional questions businesses sometimes ask. Pick any that suit you:

- What annoys you about us?
- What would we need to do in order to do more business with you?
- What disappoints you about suppliers generally?
- Which three things should we focus on to improve?
- Please sum up your impression of our business in just three words.

Step 5: The feedback

Now analyse the information. Using a rating scale of 1–5 or 1–10 allows you to summarise the customer feedback in a useful format for discussing internally.

Example

A newspaper (the customers were advertisers):
- Results by product area.
- Recruitment.
- Media buyers (key customers).

The results of Questions 1, 2 and 3 on the survey have been combined in order to provide a useful summary of the customers' perceptions.

Q1. What is important to you? (buying criteria)

Q2. Rank them in order (1–5, 1 = highest 5 = lowest).

Q3. How do you rate 'X' on the criteria?
(Scale 1–10, 1 = awful 10 = perfect)

'Good contact' – 27 customers

Rank order	1	2	3	4	5
No. of customers	7	4	7	5	4

(1 = highest 5 = lowest)

Rating	1	2	3	4	5	6	7	8	9	10
Number of customers	1	1	5	5	7	2	2	3	1	

(1 = awful 10 = perfect).

Comment: 18 out of 27 ranked this factor between 1–3 (high). Yet only 6 out of 27 rated 'X' at 8+.

'Efficiency and prompt response' – 26 customers

Rank order	1	2	3	4	5
Number of customers	5	6	7	4	4

(1 = highest, 5 = lowest)

Rating	1	2	3	4	5	6	7	8	9	10
Number of customers		1			5	1	7	8	2	2

(1 = awful, 10 = perfect).

i.e., 5 customers rated 'X' on 'Efficiency and prompt response' at 5.

Comment: 18 customers ranked this factor between 1–3. 12 customers rated 'X' at 8+ out of 26.

'Accuracy/good process/getting it right' – 16 customers

Rank order	1	2	3	4	5
Number of customers	3	4	2	6	1

(1 = highest, 5 = lowest)										
Rating	1	2	3	4	5	6	7	8	9	10
Number of customers	1		3			1	3	4	3	1

(1 = awful, 10 = perfect).
Comment: 9 customers out of 16 ranked this high. 8 out of 16 rated 'X' at 8+.

Step 6: Now take action

Take action to improve the business based upon customer feedback.

In undertaking the survey you will have raised your customers' expectations that you will be improving your service, so you had better keep your promises.

Here is an example of an action plan for the newspaper group.

Example – action plan

Many of the customers' issues reflect the improvements currently being sought and made in the ad booking and customer-service system.

The 'X' needs to ensure we provide consistent 8+ service levels in the areas identified by the customer survey:

Media buyers	Accounts personnel
Good customer support and service	Invoices correct
Good contact and communication	Good contact/communication
Accuracy/good process/ getting it right	Problems solved quickly
Adverts placed in right place	Adverts correct

The real test of the action plan is whether it consistently delivers 8+ standards of service against the criteria identified by customers. 'X' standards can be set and agreed for these service elements and included in the 'X' Newspaper way: e.g., problems resolved within 24 hours.

Specific actions that should be considered for inclusion in the 'X' Newspaper way include the following:

- Order numbers, named contact and extension number on every invoice.

- A process to ensure invoices are sent out correct to the 'X' standards:
  - Details correct
  - Order number

- Agreed standards for returning telephone calls within a given time.
- Standards agreed and set for dealing with queries quickly and effectively, e.g., within 24 hours.
- A process to ensure ads are placed in 'right place'.
- Improved quality of colour and reproduction.
- System for ensuring proofs are sent out correctly.
- A system to ensure voucher copies are sent out correctly to the right people in recruitment sector.

FOOTNOTE: The actions taken based upon the customer survey improved customer satisfaction levels from 68 to 92 per cent in three months and led to a significant boost in advertising sales to existing clients.

Conducting a customer perception survey – summary of the process

1. If you are conducting a telephone or face-to-face survey, send a letter to customers explaining what you are doing, and asking them to expect your call to arrange a mutually convenient appointment.
2. Compile the questionnaire, but keep it fairly short.
3. 'Pilot' the questions on two or three colleagues to check whether they are easy to understand and respond to.
4. Review the questions to make sure they give you the information you require.
5. Decide who is the best person to conduct the survey.
6. Make the telephone calls to arrange the face-to-face appointments.
7. Arrive on time and agree, before the meeting starts, how long you will spend with the customer, or on the call.
8. Try to obtain as much information as possible and, if a problem is uncovered, assure the customer that it will be thoroughly investigated and dealt with by your company.
9. Analyse the data.
10. Take actions to improve your business.

Troubleshooter

Potential problems	Suggested remedies
The customer information on the data used is out of date.	This happens in 95 per cent of cases. This provides an opportunity to update it before undertaking the survey.
The customers will not answer the questions.	Very rarely happens if you follow the process outlined. Customers are sometimes reluctant to discuss your competitors with you. If they do, then see this as a bonus.
Management are nervous about the feedback.	You will get balance-sheet feedback. Some credits (good things you do) and some debits (opportunities to improve).
The feedback suggests we may need to change the way we have always done business.	That's the reason for doing it.

Toolkit 17: Removing the obstacles your customers face buying from you

- Make it easy for customers to do business with you.
- Boost your sales revenue.
- Banish your 'sales prevention officers'.

Customers buy because they either want to resolve a problem or take up an opportunity. They normally expect to get something more valuable to them than the money they invest. However, companies sometimes put obstacles in the way of their customers buying from them. Here are the ten steps to helping customers to buy – steps that successful companies have used to boost their sales.

Step 1: Make the offer clear

Customers won't buy unless they clearly understand what you are offering them, so make it easy to understand your offer. Ambiguity and surprises for customers are deadly. Keep your offer simple and clear. For example, you might say, 'The package includes the holiday, flights, transport to and from the airport and all meals. There are no extra costs.' Or, 'If you can buy it cheaper anywhere else in the UK we will refund the difference. There is no small print or catches.'

Write your offer in one or two sentences.

If you can't explain it, it's highly likely that your customers will find it confusing as well, and you may well be losing sales opportunities as a result.

Step 2: Explain what's in it for them

Customers want to know what's in it for them personally. Tell them how their life will improve and why it's worth their investment. You might say, for instance, 'Undertaking our meditation programme will significantly reduce your blood pressure and anxiety. This will significantly reduce your risk of heart attack or stroke. The programme increases your life expectancy by at least ten years for £500. That's got to be a good investment.' Make something suitable for your business; this is obviously just an illustration.

List here what's in it for your customers and how their life will improve:

....

....

....

....

....

Does your offer contain the 'wow' factor? (For instance, 'When I read the benefits of meditation they made me feel like saying "Wow! I want some of this." ')

Apply the Tesco WIBIT test: Would I buy it? Tesco train all their staff to ask this question as part of their quality culture.

Manage your customers' expectations. Don't overpromise and then let customers down. In fact, do the opposite, it works wonders: underpromise, then overdeliver. Say, for example, that you'll get it to them by Friday, but deliver it much earlier.

Customers don't mind extended lead times or your problems with delivery provided that you inform them early and manage their expectations. Like you, they don't like surprises – unless they're good ones, of course!

Step 3: Deliver quickly

The faster you can deliver your product or service the more sales you will get. Customers compare your delivery performance with the fastest they get. I know it's unfair, but that's how it is. Neat Ideas grabbed a share of the office products market originally by offering 24-hour delivery. Huddersfield Ready Mix gained a 50 per cent price premium by delivering ready-mix concrete the same day. The norm was next-day delivery.

Also if a customer raises a query or requests more information to help them make a purchase decision, then provide it at lightning speed, which says to them, 'We want your business, we are keen, we will work hard on your behalf.'

How could you speed up the delivery of your product/service in order to boost your sales?

Step 4: Banish 'sales-prevention officers'!

Review your sales process through your customers' eyes. Get someone to 'mystery-shop' your business and give you feedback. Where are the 'sales-prevention officers' in your business? These are the people who make it hard for your customers to buy from you. For instance:

- Telephone operators who are rude or unhelpful to customers.
- People who don't return customers' telephone calls promptly.
- People who make it difficult for customers to do business with you.
- The nay-sayers – 'No, we can't do that ...'.

Step 5: What if they don't like your product?

Some customers won't take the risk of buying in case they don't get what they expect. Offer the best guarantee you can afford. State your guarantee clearly and in detail. An unconditional money-back guarantee will create the most sales because it eliminates all the customers' risk: no quibble – money back if not satisfied: 'If you are not delighted with our product, return it within ten days and we will give you your money back.'

What's your guarantee to your customers? Is it strong enough?

Step 6: Remove doubts

A prospective customer will not buy from you until you remove all doubt in his or her mind that you can and will deliver exactly what you promise. Testimonials are a powerful tool you can use to accomplish this. They provide proof you've that already delivered satisfaction to other customers.

Example

> ■ 'Here is a list of my existing customers. If you pick any three I will send you their telephone contacts so that you can check us out.'
>
> ■ 'Jack Jones helped us to increase our sales by 20 per cent in one year.' – Fred Smith, CEO, Space Design.

> TIP: Avoid using any claim that sounds exaggerated, even if it's true. Bold claims create doubts in customers' minds and may jeopardise the sale. Reduce any bold claims to a more believable level.

What testimonials/evidence do you provide in order to remove any doubts about you in your customers' minds? Do you have evidence to convince your customers?

Step 7: A picture's worth a thousand words ...

… but a trial is worth a thousand pictures. Get your customers to experience the product or service so they sell it to themselves. Get them to trial or try your products.

Example

> Adele McGee, who does sales training for large fashion stores, understands the benefits of encouraging women to try on clothes. 'Seventy per cent buy if you get them to try on the clothes they select. However less than 10 per cent who say they will return without trying on the clothes actually come back. The message is: get them into the changing rooms!'

Smart car salespeople try to get people to drive a car so they sell it to themselves. Advertisers put you behind the wheel of the car in their adverts.

How do you give your customers an experience of your product/service so that they sell it to themselves?

Step 8: Good reasons to buy

Customers normally make emotional decisions to purchase goods or services and they normally buy from people they like. They then search for evidence and information to confirm to themselves that they have made the right decision. Heart comes first, head comes later.

This is the time to tell them how much research went into developing your product or service. Provide them with independent evaluations and factual evidence in order to help them to justify their emotional decisions to themselves.

For example, you might say, 'There are now over three hundred independent studies that demonstrate the connection between meditation and the reduction in blood pressure.'

What evidence do you provide to your customers to help them to see that their decision was wise?

Step 9: Make it easy to buy

Did you ever walk out of a shop empty-handed rather than wait in a long queue for people to take your money? Make sure customers find it quick and easy to complete the purchase transaction. It once took thirty minutes for a salesperson to find and sell me a book in a city-centre bookstore. It took me three minutes to order the same book from Amazon.com.

How quick and easy is your sales transaction process? Look for opportunities to sell more products. For example, B&Q sales staff ask, 'Have you been able to get everything you wanted today?' Very often this leads to customers replying, 'I couldn't find X.' So they get it for the customer and sales increase by 10 per cent overall on average.

Step 10: Ask for testimonials

If you have completed Steps 1–9 so far as described in this toolkit you should have a delighted customer. So ask them for a testimonial. Use your existing delighted customers to sell to others.

Don't be afraid to ask if you have done a good job.

Summary

Make sure your buying process is simple, easy and fast. Help your customers buy from you by reviewing and acting upon these ten steps. Remember to include in your review your website and all your sales tools. Assess them rigorously. Do they meet the principles set out in this toolkit? If not, revise them so they do.

You will see an immediate increase in the number of sales you get.

Toolkit 18: Getting customer service right

- Create sustainable competitive advantage.
- Keep your customers for life.
- Deliver consistently good customer service.

It is well established that customers are five times more likely to leave because your customer service is poor than because you have poor products.

This astonishing fact puts real responsibility on businesses to get their customer service in shape.

Story – First Direct bank

First Direct pioneered telephone banking in the UK several years ago. They do all their business by telephone, so they placed great emphasis on getting their customer service right from the start. Staff were trained for several weeks in their products and processes and taught how to provide friendly helpful service before the company allowed them to speak to a 'live' customer.

They receive ongoing coaching and development from trainers who listen in to them and then review their telephone calls. You feel confident in them as a result. They are always professional and do what they say they are going to. First Direct customer service makes other banks look like dinosaurs.

Good customer services is reflected in the way you are treated as a customer from the first point of contact right through to paying your bill – and even after.

To check out your current service levels try to answer these 10 questions honestly:

1. How easy do we make it for our customers to place orders with us 24 hours a day if necessary?
2. What is our customer service promise and how well do we keep it?
3. How friendly and professional a face do we present to our customers?
4. How well do we deal with customers either on the telephone or face to face?

5. How consistent is our service morning, noon and night?
6. How do we deal with customer enquiries?
7. Are we proactive at keeping customers informed about the progress of their orders?
8. How well do we manage customer complaints?
9. How effective is our after-sales contact?
10. How many unsolicited letters of praise do we get from customers about our service?

If you can honestly answer very positively to all these questions, then you have already got your customer service right and you are now ready to delight your customers (see Toolkit 19, 'Build your business by delighting customers').

However, the majority of UK businesses in my experience will be doing well to answer three or four of these questions positively. We seem to have a problem in the UK with customer service. With a few notable exceptions, service is generally poor, which is why 67 per cent of customers quit and go to competitors.

This is your opportunity, because if you can get your service right then this might be a way to gain competitive advantage.

Here's how to do it.

Step 1: Start with your customers
Stand in their shoes and try to understand clearly what is important in terms of customer service. Visit them and ask what service standards they expect from you.

Example

Allen Johnson, chief operating officer of EWS Railway, contacted their key customers and asked them what service requirements they had.

At the time he joined the company in 1999, customers were complaining about the EWS service. Johnson got some strong messages from the customers but he was able to establish six key indicators that measured what EWS customers wanted. These included train reliability, availability, flexibility and a number of other measures.

EWS started to measure and monitor, and sought to improve the indicators. They really focused on improving the service levels. Eighteen months later their customers were delighted with their improvements in performance. All the service indicators dramatically improved.

This was during a period of real chaos after the Hatfield rail crash. This was a fantastic team performance in improving service levels in extreme conditions that most businesses never have to face.

Establish your customers' key service indicators by speaking with them. Stick to the key indicators, which may be three or four at most.

> TIP: Consider conducting a customer survey (see Toolkit 16, 'Conducting a customer perception survey', to help you to establish your key indicators).

Step 2: Measuring up

Start measuring the service indicators established in Step 1 on a monthly basis (or whatever period suits your business). This is your baseline. Things can only get better from here …

Typical service indicators might include:

- guaranteed lead times
- deliveries on time
- technical support
- 24-hour backup
- effective complaint handling
- waiting times

Step 3: Through your customers' eyes

Walk slowly and very carefully through your customer service process from first point of contact through to paying the bill. Look at the details – in great detail.

> TIP: It can be very helpful to walk, physically, through your process. Start outside your building, looking at the clarity of the signage. Walk through your premises as your customers do and see how easy you make it for them to do business with you.

> TIP: As I advised in Toolkit 17, 'Removing the obstacles your customers face buying from you', get somebody from outside your business to 'mystery-shop' your business and give you feedback. The brief is, 'How good is our customer service?'

Step 4: Six key customer interactions

The critical factor in getting customer service right is establishing a consistent approach to your customers. They don't want surprises. Here's how to do it:

1. Establish your six key customer interactions. Ask your team for help. Use this checklist for reference:

- providing a quotation
- taking a message for absent colleagues
- placing an order
- asking for a price
- chasing progress on orders
- dealing with complaints
- requesting information
- checking availability
- arranging meetings

2. Establish a small team of your people to produce a one-page, step-by-step process of your business's way of dealing with the interaction. Make sure you have customer-interfacing people who will have to use the process in their work on the design team.

This one page should use bullet points and be simple to understand. This states your preferred way of doing business. The benefits of this approach are:

- it creates consistency
- the people who use it design it, which creates ownership
- the one-page process forms the basis for induction, training, culture building and monitoring

Example: Taking a message for absent colleagues

1. Take the caller's name and company name
2. Explain your colleague is unavailable but will be available at a specified time and date
3. Ask if anybody else can help:
   a. If yes, put them through, or
   b. If no, ask if you can help in any way, or

    c. If no, then offer to take a message and pass it onto the individual. Repeat the message back to them to check the details are correct, or

    d. If it's urgent offer to get the individual to call them within 10 minutes (if they can be contacted).

4. Take their number and ask when they will be available. Promise to get your colleague to call them at an agreed time.

5. Ensure the message is passed on properly.

6. Check with your colleague that they made the call as arranged.

3. Issue the new process to everyone concerned.

4. Provide training in the process including inducting new people.

5. Set up a simple monitoring system to check it works, see Toolkit 28, 'Fixing system slippage'.

Step 5: Agreement and action

Now get your management teams together and discuss, agree and take action to improve your service levels

One of the key issues in customer service is that it is not usually one person's responsibility. Many people can have their fingerprints on the process. Customer service cuts across departments. As one MD said, 'Everybody is responsible for it but in practice nobody is responsible for it.' This is the primary reason why it proves difficult to get customer service right. Therefore, it is critical to get the real commitment of the departments in your business, and this can have a real effect on your service levels.

    ■ Review your internal customer service process.

    ■ Consider mapping your internal customer service process in order to identify if there are any blockages internally.

Example

An engineering company in the northeast England reviewed its internal customer-service process. Some salespeople took orders without getting the details absolutely correct. They passed the order on to internal production planning, which ignored the production director – there was conflict between them – and they passed the production plan to production.

The production team made the products in the order that suited them and then 'threw the products' (one of their quotes to describe the process) into dispatch, who delivered the finished product when they had transport available. Amazingly none of the departments talked together, other than to blame each other for the problems they caused. It took the MD several months of getting them together to sort out the internal customer-service chain.

Here's how to sort out internal customer service. Get department heads together and ask them to write down what they want from their internal supplier (the department before them in the internal chain) and what they think their internal customer (next in the chain) wants from them. (One MD said, 'We have more competition internally than we do with our competition externally.')

Then get them to exchange this information with each other. They will be amazed how they are making life difficult (often inadvertently, occasionally with malice) for each other. Get them to agree to some internal service standards and communications and insist they stick to them.

Review progress and ensure the internal service standards are adhered to. Be prepared to have to make some significant changes to your business structure and process in order to improve your service levels.

Examples

- EWS made cancelling trains almost a capital offence. The rule became 'Deliver on time, whatever it takes.'
- Steetley appointed customer service co-ordinators whose job it was to call customers if the deliveries of bricks were going to be late. So they kept their customers informed proactively on their deliveries.

Make sure you employ people in the front line who have good attitudes towards customers. Steetley used to hire for attitude and train for skill. I asked them how they maintained high service levels on the front line. They told me, 'Our secret's simple: we hire nice people!'

You might have to help change attitudes, fight battles or remove blockages to service in key functions such as production or finance.

Consider using Toolkit 7, 'Working on the business', as a team, to improve your service performance.

> TIP: Make sure you don't hire any sales prevention officers in the customer contact roles.

How to perfect your company service

Here is a checklist based on the latest behavioural science research on customer service. Use it with your team to perfect your service.

- Finish strong. It's not first impressions that count: it's the last impressions. The end of the service is far more important because it's what remains in your customers' recollections. Just as cruise liner trips end with dinner at the captain's table, how can you finish on a high?

- Get bad experiences out of the way early. Give the bad news early – don't delay it until the end.

- Build commitment through choice. Let customers have a choice of at least two service options – this gives them perceived ownership and control.

- Give your customers rituals and stick to them. Set up a weekly contact call, for instance, and stick to it. Rituals build trust and confidence in your service.

Step 6: Monitor and review

Continue to monitor and review your key service indicators and take action. Your indicators should be showing improvements if you have diligently taken the appropriate actions. If they are not, then plan to take some different action.

Be prepared to train front-line staff in providing good customer service.

Step 7: Communicate it!

Communicate customer-service improvements to all staff. Celebrate success, create heroes, and hold award ceremonies.

Troubleshooter

Potential problems	Suggested remedies
Customers have different needs, so it's difficult to establish generic indicators.	You need to compromise and pick 4–6 indicators that satisfy 80 per cent of all customers' needs.

We need to make changes to our business in order to really improve service levels.	Do the economics of it. Is it worth it financially in the long term? If it is, do it.
Nobody is responsible overall for customer service.	1. Make the team leaders who impact on service jointly responsible. 2. Appoint a customer-service manager with authority to manage across boundaries.
We have too much internal competition.	Consider using Toolkit 29, 'Removing process blocks and disconnects'.
It's difficult to be objective about our own service system.	Get a third party to 'mystery-shop' your business and give you honest feedback.

Toolkit 19: Build your business by delighting customers

- Increase customer loyalty, get new customers from referrals and reduce price sensitivity.
- Build competitive advantage.
- Grow your business profitability.

Delighting customers means doing that bit extra for customers in order to create customer satisfaction beyond the norm.

If it is done well, it can lead to high levels of repeat business, new opportunities coming from referrals from delighted customers and a lowering of sensitivity to price.

Delighting customers is more than just good customer service. Making it easy to place an order, treating them with respect, getting queries answered and goods delivered on time does not delight customers: this is *basic customer service*. It's a right, not a delight.

Delighting customers has the following additional qualities over basic customer service:

1. Something spontaneous or unexpected

Example

A private hospital was averaging 56 per cent on its patient-satisfaction ratings. In order to boost its ratings the hospital rang each patient one week prior to their operation to check if they were OK and had any questions or concerns.

The call was repeated one week after the patient was discharged. The calls were courtesy, not medical. Within one month the patient-satisfaction ratings rose from 56 to 85 per cent, a 50 per cent improvement, and stayed there. It's amazing what showing genuine interest in your customers can achieve.

2. Speed of delivery

Here's an opportunity to give customers a pleasant surprise. Deliver their goods with a breathtaking speed of response. Have them saying, 'They said expect delivery in three days and it arrived within hours!'

3. Outstanding attention to detail

Example

The Four Seasons Hotel in Chicago asked my secretary lots of detailed questions when she booked me a room. As well as the usual questions, such as whether I wanted a smoking or non-smoking room, they asked whether I liked a hard or soft bed, whether I wanted flowers in the room, whether I'd like my suit pressed overnight, whether they could collect me from the airport. The details seemed endless …

When I arrived they delivered exactly what I wanted. The attention to detail was superb. But the best bit was when I visited the Four Seasons in Hawaii: they provided exactly the same service. How? My details were on their database, so I now get what I want every time without asking. Now *that's* customer delight!

4. Problem solving beyond the norm

Example

Ellen, my partner, often complained that, while her hairdresser did her hair perfectly, within hours it was often wrecked, particularly if the wind was blowing. This is a problem for many women, particularly if they visit the hairdresser in the morning and are then attending a function later in the evening. It never quite looks as good.

Ellen's hairdresser responded to her problem by doing her hair, then undoing it and teaching Ellen how to re-create the style herself exactly as it should be. This was problem solving beyond the norm.

5. Showing genuine personal interest

Example

'You said you're interested in visiting Hollywood on your trip, so I've been on the Internet and got some information that might help you. I've researched the best restaurants, car hire, opening times of the major attractions you said you were interested in, with contact names and telephone numbers. I contacted the car-hire people and arranged for you to pick one up at the airport without queuing for two hours.'

Makes you feel good and important, doesn't it? Or how about, 'Mr Hall, we arranged for a personal car-parking bay for you when you visit us'?

Here are three example benefits enjoyed by businesses that have delighted their customers:

- 'Our customer-delight approach means we are now able to negotiate rather than tender for most of our work – this has improved our margins.' (Dick Watson, Keepmoat PLC.)
- 'We set out to delight our customers from Day One and consequently 80 per cent of our customers are regulars. They also recommend us to their friends and colleagues. We have never had to spend money on marketing or advertising.' (Stephen King, Ye Olde Sun Inn Restaurant.)
- 'We charge twice the price of our nearest competitors because we delight our customers and their animals.' (Ann Adlington, Triple 'A' Ranch.)

Here is a story to illustrate how customer delight exceeds customer service. We had carpets fitted on two separate occasions. Carpet fitter A did it to the very minimum customer-service standards. Carpet fitter B delighted us by exceeding our expectations. We can compare from the six points of contact how A and B performed.

1. **A** suggested we visit their shop to look at some samples.

   B delivered his carpet samples to our home within one hour of our initial contact (speed and different from the norm).

2. **A** extolled the virtues of a new carpet, which was 'selling like hot cakes'.

   B asked us about our colour scheme. Did we need a hard-wearing carpet? How long did we plan to stay (no point in investing in good carpets if you are moving in twelve months)? And there were a host of other very detailed questions, which suggested he was really interested in helping us make the right choice for us, not him. Nothing seemed to be too much trouble. (Personal touch, attention to detail, warm and friendly, different from the norm.)

3. **A** said the carpets would be delivered in the next two weeks.

   B said they would be delivered to his shop next Tuesday and then asked, 'Would it be convenient to fit them on Wednesday at eight a.m.?' He confirmed all this in a short letter with contact numbers to check details (attention to detail).

4. **A** said he would fit the carpets sometime on Wednesday morning. He called on Wednesday morning to say he was running late and would Thursday be OK?

   B turned up at the appointed time to fit the carpets. He rang the night before to confirm all the details (attention to detail).

5. **A** fitted the carpets but left the offcuts for us to clear away. The carpet fitters worked at lightning speed without speaking, other than the occasional grunt. Was this a quick and nasty job? Did we trust them? Did they care?

   B was warm and friendly and explained what he was doing in some detail. He made us feel the fitters were highly professional, knew what they were doing and intended to do a quality job. We trusted them. (Warm and friendly, attention to detail.)

6. **A** left without a word when the fitters had finished.

   B explained how to look after the carpet and even recommended the best vacuum cleaner. The fitters even left a small vase with some flowers and a card that read, 'Mrs Hall, welcome to your new home, from the carpet fitters'. (Beyond expectations, put a smile on our faces, spontaneous.)

The results of these two quite different experiences were:

- We actively discouraged people from using A.
- We have used B to fit all our carpets over the past fifteen years. We have recommended them to at least ten other people.
- B was more expensive than A but we believe the premium is well worth it.

This was customer delight in living colour. Customer delight may or may not come from one piece of outstanding service, or it can be a combination of several pleasant surprises that add up to delighting customers.

Story – Bonar Flotex

'Can you come and meet us? We're interested in your idea about delighting customers.' This was the request from Peter Bartlett, CEO of Bonar Flotex in Derbyshire.

The following day an AA route map arrived giving exact directions from my office to Bonar Flotex (not the usual illegible faxed copy of a photocopied map that looks like a black blob).

I turned up at their factory and the security guard on the gate greeted me with a warm smile with 'Good morning, Mr Hall. Park your car over there.' (How did he know who I was?) He pointed to a reserved car-parking spot next to reception with a sign that read RESERVED FOR MR DAVID HALL. My normal experience is that these are generally reserved for the company's directors, occasionally with a sign: IF YOU PARK HERE YOUR CAR WILL BE CLAMPED.

As I entered reception the receptionist smiled and greeted me very warmly, 'Good morning, Mr Hall. Did you have a good journey? Here's your badge. Please take a seat.' (How did she know who I was?) Again, this is not the norm: in my experience you are usually asked to fill in a form by an often busy receptionist.

As I took my seat a door opened and a young man arrived with a black coffee – Colombian (my favourite) – and two chocolate biscuits. 'Good morning, Mr Hall. Mr Bartlett will be with you in two and a half minutes.' (How did he know who I was?)

This was getting beyond belief. I was half expecting Jeremy Beadle to appear! How did they know I had black coffee and chocolate biscuits at 10.30 every morning?

By now I was timing them but at 10.30 a.m. precisely, as suggested, Bartlett appeared and showed me into his office. I thought, I'll find a crack in this amazing customer-delight experience. So I asked how good they really were at service with their real customers? He turned to his computer and said, 'Let's start with delivery. Do you want year to date, this month or this week?' Year to date 98.4 per cent, this month 99.6 per cent. 'Oh, OK,' I said, 'I surrender. How do you do it?'

'Well we got the team together and we brainstormed how we could delight our customers. The team had loads of ideas because they are dealing with customers all the time. So we developed their customer-delight ideas. For example, when a new customer or contact is coming to visit us my secretary calls theirs and finds out their car registration number and how they take their beverages, and we write it in a book and communicate it to everybody. Simple stuff but it blows customers' brains out.'

It certainly impressed me, but the real point is that ten years later I have purchased Bonar Flotex kitchen carpets every time I have moved house and have recommended them to dozens of people – and *that's* the real point.

'Customer delight really does work – try it,' says Peter Bartlett.

So let us explore how you can create customer delight in *your* business.

Step 1: Check on the system

Ensure your basic customer-service system is operating effectively (see Toolkit 18, 'Getting customer service right'). You will not delight customers unless your basic customer-service system is sound and consistent.

> TIP: Check for any sales-prevention officers in your business and keep them away from your customers.

Step 2: Brainstorm opportunities

Get your team together and explain that you want to build your business by delighting your customers. (See also Toolkit 7, 'Working on the business'.)

Brainstorm opportunities to delight your customers from the initial point of contact with them right through the business transaction until they pay the bill. Use the ingredients checklist (A) to help people recognise delighting opportunities. Use the customer-delight checklist (B) to provide ideas and inspiration to your team.

Checklist A
The ingredients of customer delight
Go beyond their expectations
Be spontaneous
Add a personal touch
Give speed of response
Demonstrate attention to detail
Make them feel important
Put a smile on their face
Be warm and friendly
Show you're different from the norm

Checklist B
Ideas for delighting customers
Send an AA route map to help them find your office
Allocate a car-parking slot with their name on for their visit
Put their name on a board in reception
Personally greet them at reception
Send a thank-you note personally written
Get and use their first name often
Treat them like a best friend
Introduce them personally to your team
Do something for them at lightning speed, such as sending a quote within the hour by email
Give them your undivided attention
Focus on the details
Give them a company gift – tie, mug etc.
Take them out to dinner
Find out what interests them and provide it

Offer to introduce them to your network
Solve a problem for them
Hire people who are good with customers

Step 3: Stimulate creativity

Help to stimulate your team's creative thinking about customer delight by getting them to talk with and learn from those businesses that really do delight customers. For example:

- Get people to talk to First Direct, the telephone bank, and see how they are treated.
- Visit any Four Seasons Hotel in the world and see how they delight customers.
- Take them to a really good restaurant as a team to see how they delight customers.
- Find out in your area who delights customers really well and arrange for your team to visit them.

Step 4: Gather ideas

Collect all their ideas on a flipchart. Decide which is only *good* customer service and which is likely to *delight* your customers.

Agree the customer-delight elements. Get everyone to agree to delight customers and set up a system to ensure customers are constantly delighted. (See the example of Bonar Flotex above.)

> TIP: Ask customers how they found your service and feed the delight examples back to your team to reinforce the process.

> TIP: Put delighting customers on to your meeting agendas and constantly seek new ideas to keep the process fresh.

Step 5: Get feedback

Conduct regular customer feedback sessions to establish how consistently you are delighting customers. Feed back the results with a sincere 'well done' to everyone.

Step 6: See for yourself

Inspect your customer delight process yourself. Try to see your business through your customers' eyes to ensure no system slippage.

Get a trusted friend to 'mystery-shop' your business on your behalf.

Step 7: Monitoring

Make sure your customer information system monitors the effect of delighting customers.

Calculate the level of repeat business as a percentage of sales. It should be over 80 per cent. Record the source of new business, for instance, the level of referrals.

Nudge your prices up to test your customers' reaction. This is the acid test: are they delighted enough to pay more?

CHAPTER SIX

Creating Sales

Toolkits 20–22

Toolkit 20: Build your business by networking
Toolkit 21: Problem seeking, problem solving, to create opportunities
Toolkit 22: Increasing sales using the turnover drivers

Toolkit 20: Build your business by networking

- Create and maintain relationships with people who can help you build your business.
- Obtain information and resources at low cost.
- Open doors to new opportunities.

Networking is about building and maintaining relationships with people who can help you achieve your business goals. No business has all the resources or information it requires internally. Therefore, you need to forge strong links with people who can help you.

In numerous studies, networking, building alliances and making connections has been shown to be the major contributor to successful business growth and development.

Networking is not about attending as many business lunches or business clubs as possible, that's usually '*not* working'! It is about identifying those people, including people in other departments in your business, who can help you to develop your business, and then building and maintaining a positive relationship with them so that they will provide help and support when you need it, such as

- Contacts with target customers.
- Providing invaluable market intelligence.
- Access to resources including finance.
- Help to remove blockages to progress.
- Giving your business much greater reach and influence.
- Creating new profitable business.
- People in other departments in your business with whom it is important to collaborate rather than compete.

Let's look at two stories that clearly demonstrate different aspects of networking.

Story – Jo Sneddon

Jo Sneddon set up a new consultancy practice in Perth, Australia, in 1999. Jo was new to the city and consequently had few contacts or established networks.

'I attended every Chamber of Commerce lunch and business breakfast going. This was very time-consuming and did not create many new opportunities for me. Eventually, I realised that I was not networking with the people who could provide me with business leads and contacts, so I started afresh. I asked myself, Who do I really want to do business with and who influences them?

'I quickly realised that the key signposters were business development people at the local government agency, regional managers of the banks responsible for medium and large clients and conference organisers.

'So I set out to make a list of the key people in Perth in these three categories and started visiting them and establishing relationships.

'I found that the government agency people had databases of local businesspeople, which I could access. They also introduced me to a number of their clients because I did some free market research for them in order to help them identify new targets. They were delighted and went out of their way to help.

'The banks looked like a good networking contact, but I found they were very reluctant to introduce me to their clients and never actually did!

'However, the conference organisers turned out to be my best network contacts. I developed some marketing and PR material that helped them boost their sales for free, so they gave me their contact lists and also invited me to speak at some of their conferences. This turned out to be a real win–win.

'Networking really helped me build my business and we have never looked back since. We still network but do it in a much more targeted way.'

JO'S TIP: Network with people who can really help you.

Story – Simon Woodroffe, Yo Sushi

Simon Woodroffe worked in the music and TV business with some of the biggest names in pop as his clients. Yet he felt frustrated. One of his Japanese clients said, 'What you should do, Simon, is to set up a conveyor-belt sushi bar.' So Simon decided that was what he would do.

But he had two major problems: he knew nothing about running a food outlet and even less about sushi – not a great start.

'So I started calling people up,' he says, 'but many dismissed me unceremoniously. I networked my way round London using all my old contacts. I thought who could help me raise the money. I made a list and then started to network with them. I also saw site after site and at every rejection I had to remind myself that this was taking me closer to my goal.

'I also had to network by telephone into Japan, at eight pounds a minute, in order to find out how sushi bars worked. Eventually a guy sent me a manual on how to run a sushi bar with everything in it! Fantastic. I also used my contacts to get me into Honda and Sony. It took twelve months of constant networking and effort. Eventually they agreed to sponsor me. We put their names on our restaurant door and people said that if Honda and Sony are sponsoring them then they must be a big player!

'Simple formulas really. Network constantly and eventually you will get what you want. Once I realised that you had to build and maintain relationships with people and that rejection is not personal then I created more chances to score a goal.'

SIMON'S TIP: Be brave, pick up the phone and expect to be rejected seven times at least – but be persistent.

So how should you go about networking?

Step 1: Determine what you need
Decide what help you need to assist you in building your business. Do you need help to get:

- finance?
- new customers?
- information?
- competitor knowledge?
- resources?
- ongoing intelligence?
- technical information?
- market information?
- positive PR?
- others?

Summarise your needs here:

1.

2.

3.

4.

5.

6.

TIP: If you don't complete Step 1 then you can waste a lot of time networking with people who cannot help. Dinah Bennett, an expert in networking, reckons that if you do not target your networking you may need to meet fifty people to get what you want. Targeted networking reduces the contact rate to ten people – a 500 per cent improvement.

Step 2: Decide whom you need

Determine who could help you to build your business by meeting the needs you have identified. Write them in the table below. Don't be afraid to ask around to see who can help you.

Needs	Key network contacts
1.	
2.	
3.	
4.	
5.	
6.	

Get to know 'signposters', who are people with extensive networks themselves who could signpost you to the right contact. Try to identify:

- experts – people who have the knowledge you really need
- key players – influential figures who could help
- industry leaders – often have extensive networks and can open doors for you
- helpers – people who are paid to help people like you

Seek advice from others in your industry – whom do they find helpful. Make a list of key network contacts.

> TIP: Remember, it's not organisations that are helpful but the good people who work for them.

Step 3: Making contact

Try to find out the best way to contact the people on your contact list. Whom do you know who might introduce you to them? What networks do they belong to?

Do your homework on your key contacts. Work out how to contact them and what you might say to them.

> TIP: You are often only three phone calls away from the person you want. In other words, you know somebody well who has a friend who knows your target contact well.

Step 4: Interpersonal skills

Develop your interpersonal skills, so that when you contact people you do it in a skilful way in order to maximise your chances of success (see Toolkit 4, 'Being interpersonally skilled').

Step 5: Approach your contacts

Approach your network contacts and take an interest in them. Get to know them – do something for them.

Invite them to dinner or a sponsored event, golf or races. Ask them what they like doing and delight them.

Step 6: Obey the rules

Observe the rules of good networking when dealing with your key contacts. Start giving before you need to receive. Acknowledge others' contributions publicly – share the limelight.

Don't burn your bridges. Don't whinge, complain or gossip maliciously to people in your network.

Get in touch with your contacts often, not just when you want something – and remember to thank people for any help they provide. Recognise that networking is a two-way process.

Try to create 'significant moments' for people in your network. The first time I visited my friend Gerard Egan in Chicago he took me for dinner with his friends – he had arranged for the restaurant to print book matches for everyone with my name on. A significant moment!

Step 7: Make your network work for you

Put your contacts in your forward contact system. Contact them regularly and frequently with news, information, help or intelligence. Try to contact them every three months as a minimum, not just when you need their help.

If you ask for help and they respond, then always say thank you. As Tom Peters, the leading American management guru, said, 'If you want to build your business, send thank-you notes.'

Step 8: Don't spread yourself too thinly

If you are intending to attend an event where you might want to network with a range of new people, decide who looks the most promising and concentrate upon one or two people. Don't give out thirty business cards to just anybody, hoping you might strike gold.

Practise your introduction and be interesting: 'I'm John Smith. I'm here to meet people who might be interested in doing business in Japan ...'

Step 9: Work at it

Keep working at it. Make networking a key part of your role.

Our research shows that in businesses that successfully grow and develop, the managing director or senior management are spending at least 50 per cent of their time outside the business networking with key contacts.

Toolkit 21: Problem seeking, problem solving, to create opportunities

- Get really close to your customers.
- Create new profitable business opportunities.
- Build sustainable competitive advantage.

Talking to customers is good, listening to them is better, but spending time in their environment, trying to understand their world and how your product or service is used in practice, is one of the best ways to create new opportunities.

By being able actually to use your own products or service in the environment they were designed to operate in, you get to discover the problems and opportunities your product or services create for your customers. So, while you're there, make sure you always ask the right questions.

Story – Engine Component Distributor

'We accompanied one of our customers on a site visit when they were installing one of our replacement parts in a tractor. We soon found that our packaging was too bulky for them on site, and that the accompanying installation instructions were useless. The engineers said they'd grumbled regularly to their boss about them, but this had never been passed on to us. We sorted it quickly. We increased our business with them by 60 per cent in three months.'

The process is called problem seeking, problem solving. Here is an overview of the process.

1. You deliberately immerse yourself in your customer's business in order to experience your product in use. The process works because you see at first hand what needs to be done to help. Sometimes customers have difficulty in describing their needs (the classic marketing approach). Problem seeking, problem solving cuts right through that problem. Clearly, you should select some big-opportunity customers to spend time with where it is worth the effort.

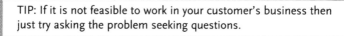

TIP: If it is not feasible to work in your customer's business then just try asking the problem seeking questions.

2. You ask good questions while you are with them and problems will emerge.

3. These problems become your opportunities. You help your customers solve their problems by using/adapting your products or services.

4. You develop a solution to their problem and fix it fast! Fixing it quickly is what creates surprised and delighted customers.

5. If you solve their problems quickly you could enjoy the ultimate reward of problem seeking, problem solving, and that is a 'friend for life'. This forms the basis for long-term business partnerships.

Story – Stationery Business, London

A stationery supplier delivered to hospitals and offices across London. The sales director was well into the process of problem seeking, problem solving, which helped him to discover that many of his customers wanted delivery just in time but frequently ran out of supplies. The problem was that it was often difficult to deliver just in time during the day in London because of traffic congestion. So he decided that their core competency was delivery, not stationery, and started to deliver between the hours of midnight and 6 a.m. He also found that their customers had a problem getting supplies of some basic commodities such as toilet rolls, cleaning materials and laundry.

The roads were quiet at that time and they found that they could deliver four times the quantities they could during daylight hours!

The customers' problems were solved, so they were delighted and started placing more orders for an increasingly diverse range of supplies. This transformed the business.

Problem seeking, problem solving = more business!

Here's how to do it.

Step 1: Identify target customers

Identify some target customers with whom you want to do more business because:

- You have a small share of their spend.
- They are growing fast and you want to piggyback on their success.
- You want to become their preferred supplier.

Step 2: Work with them

Use your contacts in your customer's business to get permission to spend some time working in their business using your product or service.

A friend of mine wanted to sell more of his cleaning materials to some NHS trusts. He volunteered to work with the cleaning team and worked as a porter for two days. He identified four new cleaning-product opportunities from his range, which the NHS were happy to buy from him. They trusted him and really appreciated the time and effort he took in trying to understand their problems at the sharp end. Friend for life!

Step 3: Be alert

While you are working in your customer's environment keep your eyes and ears open:

- What problems do they have?
- Watch carefully how they are using your product/service.

- Are they getting the best out of it?
- How could you adapt your product/service to make it easier for them to use?
- What other problems do they have that you might be able to help them resolve?
- Would the staff benefit from some training in the use of your product or service?

Example

A brick-manufacturing company wanted to increase their sales with one of the UK's largest builders' merchants. A salesperson spent three days in a customer's merchant branch and was horrified to find that the staff didn't understand the difference between types of bricks, which could create severe construction problems.

He provided some training for the customer sales team and solved the problem.

If you can't get into working with the customer, just ask the problem-seeking questions in Step 4. It is not as powerful as working with them but it should produce some interesting opportunities.

Step 4: Ask problem-seeking questions

Here is a sample of some of the problem-seeking questions you might find it useful to ask. Adapt them to suit your own particular circumstances.

- What problems do you currently face?
- How do you find our product/service?
- Is this typically how you would use it?
- What do you like about it?
- What do you dislike about it?
- What would make it easier for you?
- What improvements would you like to see in your business?
- What are your priorities right now?

Step 5: Create solution

Once you have identified customer problems, it's time to create solutions. Start by reviewing the customer's problems. For example, ask:

- How easy do they find it to buy from you?
- Do they get the technical support they need?
- How well do your products/services really solve their problems?
- How well trained are they in using your products/services?

Seek to identify problems that will give you a quick result – for instance, one that might have you saying, 'We'll send a confirmation of your order to help sort out your internal and admin problems.'

Do a cost/benefit analysis of some of the issues.

Step 6 Fix things fast!

You create your desired status of 'friend for life' by fixing things at lightning speed. Pull out all the stops to surprise and delight your customers with your speed of reaction.

They will probably be used to normal supplier speed – 'dead slow or reverse' – so stand out from the crowd and gain competitive edge.

Example

Haslam Consulting of Glasgow was asked to quote for a large market research contract. During the sales meeting the customer mentioned that he was generally disappointed with the slow response to their requests. 'You would think they didn't want our business sometimes.' Simon Haslam, the principal of Haslam Consulting, took the hint and personally delivered the quotation for the work within four hours. 'The customer was amazed by our speed of response and we got the contract.'

Toolkit 22: Increasing sales using the turnover drivers

- Use the six turnover drivers to really boost sales.
- Reduce the feast-or-famine impact of fluctuating sales.
- Establish an effective business-generating system.

There are only six ways to increase sales in any business. Successful businesses set up sales systems to use the six sales drivers to boost their business. The drivers are:

- creation of new sales prospects
- improved conversion rates, e.g., quotes to order

- improved retention rate of existing customers
- increased transaction value of each sale
- increased transaction frequency of each sale
- improved frequency of customer visits

Story – Fone Zone, Queensland, Australia

Six years ago a former sales executive, David McMahon, and his partner, Maxine Horne, began a mobile-phone retail business in Queensland with the 'naïve' notion that it would provide them with independence, an income and a better lifestyle.

Instead, the pair, who hedged their inexperience at running a business by borrowing ideas from the United Kingdom, found themselves leading a high-velocity retail revolution.

The catalyst for their early growth, beyond the dynamics of the market itself, was being the first to put mobile-phone retail outlets within the reach of everyday consumers in shopping centres and malls.

Fone Zone, with 46 outlets, is now the country's largest independent mobile-phone retailer. It had profit growth of 22 per cent in the year 2000 and ranks as one of Australia's fastest-growing private companies.

'When we realised the business was going to grow so fast, we had to sit down and learn the basic principles of how to run it,' says McMahon, the company's CEO. 'We were starting from scratch with the business plan and spent eighteen months educating ourselves in retail management.

'The greatest awakening in the process was discovering turnover drivers. It's relatively simple, really: there are only six areas of a business you can focus on to increase sales and turnover. For me it was a true dawning. Everything stems from understanding the equation. It's too easy to think that because sales are down you must advertise, when you may need to improve the conversion rate of your prospects.

'It's not until these measurements are in place that a business can be improved. Accordingly, systems have been established in all stores so, at the press of a button each morning, the business owners can see how each is performing in all six areas, and fine-tune.'

Now positioned for the rapid growth of WAP and data-based information services (it is predicted that by 2004 more people will access the web by mobile phone or wireless device than PC), the company will undertake a public float in 2001.

Step 1: Set up a monitoring system

Yes, I know that monitoring is normally the final step in most business processes but not in this one. You need to monitor your current existing performance against the six drivers in order to identify opportunities for improvement.

Delegate the task to a competent person to set up an effective monitoring system, preferably using your computer system or a PC.

You need constantly to monitor your performance in order to identify areas for development. The information manager's role is a crucial one, so don't compromise and give it to a weak resource.

Here are some tips on how they might do it.

1. Create new sales prospects

This requires that all sales personnel record very accurately the source of new leads and prospects. Make it a mantra: Get the sale and get the source of the sale.

Put the information on to the sales order entry format. Audit the process frequently to ensure that your people are recording accurate information.

2. Conversion rates

These might be:

- marketing effort to leads: e.g., ten enquiries for each advert and 5 per cent replies from mailshots
- lead to quotes: e.g., four leads provides us with two opportunities to quote (50 per cent)
- quote to orders: e.g., we win one order per three quotes (ratio is 1:3)

Give the sales-management function the responsibility for calculating and recording the conversion rates accurately.

3. Retention rate of existing customers

Check sales records and invoices on a regular basis. Where does our business come from? Crucially, how much from existing customers?

4. Transaction value of each order

Check sales orders and invoices in order to calculate average order size (total sales value divided by orders received). You might need to establish a common process for calculating average order size particularly if your sales invoices carry a range of items.

5. Transaction frequency

Monitor transaction frequency via the sales order system. How often do our customers buy?

6. Customer visits

Make the information resource person responsible for co-ordinating diaries and visits to customers.

Most of this information already exists. The information resource person needs the support of the IT function to enable them to access the data from the existing system.

Step 2: Analyse data

Once the monitoring system is established and running smoothly for a period of, say, three months, then begin to analyse the data and start to ask some questions:

- Where do our new customers actually come from?
- How effective is our business-generating system at creating the quantity and quality of customers?
- How effective are our conversion rates?
- Do conversion rates vary and why?
- How well do we keep existing customers?
- What is the average transaction value?
- Is it increasing or decreasing?
- How often do our customers buy?
- Do we visit our customers often enough?

You should find this analysis very revealing.

> TIP: Involve your sales team in the process to ensure they buy in to the plans for improvement.

Step 3: Improve the drivers

Discuss and agree sales and marketing tasks to improve the drivers.

> TIP: This whole toolkit is driven by the installation of an accurate and effective data-recording system. Do not compromise the quality of the data capture – the benefits are worth it.

Here are some things you could do:

Driver 1: Creating new customers
Cut your spend on your marketing methods that your new information tells you are not working. Increase your spend on those methods that are proven to work.

Example

A caravan dealer in the Midlands was spending £100k on creating new prospects. (Driver 1, 'Create new sales prospects'). Analysis of the sales monitoring system after three months revealed that 80 per cent of new customers came from *Yellow Pages* advertising, which cost the business £3k.

Their plan was to reduce their marketing spend by £90k with no negative impact on creating new customers.

They also found that events such as barbecues on a weekend created new customers but they had done only two in the year. They decided to spend £7k on several special barbecue weekends and created significant numbers of new customers.

Driver 2: Conversion rates
The key issues normally are:

- Are we attracting the right target customers to sell to?
- How good is our offer?
- How effective are our salespeople at selling?

You can audit these issues by talking to a sample of customers and asking them about your offer. You can watch your salespeople sell in order to assess their effectiveness.

Whatever you find take action to fix it.

Driver 3: Improve the retention rate of existing customers
Conduct a customer perception survey (see toolkit 16) in order to find out why customers stay and leave.

Remember your sales tactics with existing customers. What do we do to keep them? What can we improve? Should we offer a gold star service to key customers?

Driver 4: Increasing transaction values

Consider auditing your cross-selling process. How effective is it?

In the 1980s Mothercare's average order size was £4.75. They worked at improving the merchandising around the checkouts and increased it to £5.50. This boosted their profits significantly.

Ask, 'Do we offer our customers our full range in order to increase our transaction sale?' Set up a system to improve cross-selling, if one does not exist.

Driver 5: Increase the frequency of each sale

Consider special offers to increase the frequency of sales, including a loyalty scheme.

Or you might consider offering telesales to increase the frequency. You could try offering a gold-star service to existing customers to increase transaction sales. Brainstorm some ideas internally.

> TIP: Be careful about giving anything away via discounts. You want to increase your profits as well as your sales.

Driver 6: Increase the frequency of customer visits

In fast-growth companies top people spend 30–50 per cent of their time networking with their customers. The rewards are lots of new sales opportunities.

Get your top team to commit to a minimum number of days per month to visit customers. Encourage your information-resource person to record their visits to enable you to monitor progress.

Troubleshooter

Potential problems	Suggested remedies
Can't release anybody internally to act as the information resource person. Or ... They are too busy with other projects and the job does not get done.	Remember the potential benefit to your business: a significant boost to sales. Therefore, make finding the right resource person a number-one priority.
The IT department have too many projects, so they cannot help. (This seems to be a major blockage in every large business.)	1. Make it the priority for them. 2. Outsource it to an agency.

People do not provide accurate input data (e.g., source of new leads).	You need to make it mandatory in your business. Remember the rewards ...
There's a tendency to blame external factors, rather than internal performance, for less than satisfactory sales performance.	Accurate data should identify where the real problems exist.

CHAPTER SEVEN

Developing New Products and Services

 Toolkits 23–24

Toolkit 23: 'Intrepreneurship': innovate and reinvent your business
Toolkit 24: Developing a superior product or service

 Toolkit 23: 'Intrepreneurship': innovate and reinvent your business

- Bring Silicon Valley into your business.
- Create new existing products and services.
- Unleash the entrepreneurial and innovative spirit in your business.

Many businesses are now facing increasing price and product competition. The once sure-footed step of the gazelle has been replaced by the plodding gait of the dinosaur. These businesses find it increasingly difficult to innovate, renew and reinvent themselves.

Story – 3M Innovation

3M Innovation are often held up as a good example of a company who have been successful at innovation by encouraging 'intrepreneurship' within their business. They work very hard at it.

Seven per cent of their annual sales of £17 billion dollars is spent on technology building, and 85 per cent of that is devoted to new product development. They maintain the level of spending regardless of profit trends in the business. They encourage anybody in the business to spend 15 per cent of their time working on their own ideas in work time. Innovation in 3M is described as the commercialisation of ideas, not just inventing for its own sake.

They have created a culture where people have the right to fail – it's OK to make mistakes. They are 'intrepreneurs' in the way they develop and extend their products.

Take Post-it notes as an example. By watching how their customers used Post-it notes they realised that often when answering the phone you cannot pull off a note to write a message, so they developed the one-handed dispenser. They also realised that their sticky tape was made in rolls to suit them, not the customer. Can you ever find the end of Scotchtape? So they developed the wrist dispenser for wrapping presents.

They also share technology and ideas right across the business and leverage new technology and ideas into every part of the business (see Toolkit 25, 'Using the EntreNet to really boost your business').

Yet there is a hard business edge to all they do. They set tough targets for innovation. Twenty-five per cent of all sales must come from products that have been launched within the past four years. This is a magnificent business that has put innovation at the top of its agenda and even included it in its brand name.

Many of the traditional approaches to creating an internal entrepreneurial, innovative culture have not produced the desired results.

What has been learned about trying to create this in an existing business might be called 'intrepreneurial'.

How *not* to create an 'intrepreneurial' culture

- Set up a 'special projects' team of 'volunteers'.
- Insist on measurable outcomes or objectives.
- Meet monthly.
- Appoint people to the team who have the time to be there.
- Insist on regular detailed reports and updates.
- Establish detailed screening criteria for new ideas.

- Throw money at the problem.
- Encourage the innovation team to be different – e.g., dress down Wednesday mornings and all day Friday.
- Innovate behind closed doors, keeping customers in the dark in case your competitors discover what you are doing.
- Set out to create a 'culture of innovation'.

Many of the attempts to encourage 'intrepreneurship' may have faltered because they contravene the ways entrepreneurs actually do innovate and create value.

Therefore, it might be helpful to summarise the latest findings about how entrepreneurs do their work (the fundamental laws of entrepreneurship) and then try to apply these lessons internally to create '*intre*preneurship'.

1. Entrepreneurship is now generally defined as 'creating value often from practically nothing'. It is a resource-light activity, so throwing money at it may well be counterproductive.

2. Entrepreneurship is a creative act requiring vision, passion and obsessive commitment. It is mainly a right-brain, creative, intuitive process, so setting up committees and insisting on detailed reports (typical left-brain planning and control processes) almost certainly do not add value to the creative entrepreneurial process. In fact they inhibit it.

3. The three key drivers of entrepreneurial behaviour are:

Spotting opportunities

Marshalling resources   Building capability

Most entrepreneurial acts start with spotting an opportunity to solve a customer problem or becoming more efficient and effective internally.

Entrepreneurs rarely have all the resources to take up the opportunity and it is this tension between opportunity and lack of resources that creates the energy to make it work – 'comrades in adversity', as one entrepreneur put it.

Building the capability to take up the opportunity often involves recruiting the right skills into a team or learning quickly from others, building alliances or partnerships and developing the culture.

4. Inventors are obsessed with their ideas. Entrepreneurs turn ideas into a product, which solves a customer problem, and in doing so create a valued business. The implication is that entrepreneurship is a customer-focused activity, so involve customers right from the start of the process.

5. Entrepreneurs' qualities are different from business skills:

Entrepreneurial qualities – example (right-brain)	Business skills – example (left-brain)
Networking	Planning
Obsessive commitment	Decision making
Tolerating ambiguity	Time management
Taking responsibility	

6. Entrepreneurs learn how to create value in ways that are different from those in which traditional business management is taught.

Entrepreneurial learning (right-brain)	Traditional business teaching (left-brain)
Just doing it	Courses
From successful peers	Books
Family and friends	'Experts'

Business skills can be taught, but we do not yet know how to 'teach' entrepreneurial qualities.

7. Entrepreneurs develop their recipe for success by synthesising information from whatever source is appropriate or they personally deem credible. Business is usually taught as an analytical process, breaking the problem down into manageable steps. So one is pulling together and building while the other is pulling apart and deconstructing.

If you compare some of the traditional ways of trying to encourage 'intrepreneurship' by large organisations with the fundamental laws of entrepreneurship, it's not difficult to see why many attempts at 'intrepreneuring' have failed.

If you need any more convincing, consider these three facts:

- 95 per cent of all the innovations up to 1991 in radical new products and services came from businesses employing fewer than 20 people. (Source: D Birch, EfER [European Foundation for Entrepreneurial Research] Conference, Berlin, 1991.)

- 50 per cent of all fast-growth businesses are run by people who worked for large companies, got disillusioned by the corporate culture, left and set up their own business. (Source: John Case, 'The Origins of Entrepreneurship', *Inc.*, June 1989.)

- In the majority of successful start-up businesses, the lead entrepreneur has spent at least ten years serving an apprenticeship. This includes understanding the technology and the players in the industry, building network contacts and learning how the business works. (Source: Karl H Vesper, 'New Venture Ideas: Don't overlook the entrepreneurial factor', *Harvard Business Review*, 1984.)

So how can existing businesspeople successfully apply the fundamental laws of entrepreneurship in their organisation in order to encourage 'intrepreneurship'?

We know that entrepreneurs synthesise ideas rather than slavishly follow rules and guidelines, so pick the bits that suit you in order to create your own way of doing things. (Note that the steps in this toolkit are not necessarily sequential.)

Here's how to do it.

Step 1: Start thinking and acting as an entrepreneur

Talk to entrepreneurs in order to imbibe some of their attitudes, beliefs and qualities. Read books on entrepreneurship mentioned in the bibliography, such as my *In the Company of Heroes – An insider's guide to entrepreneurs at work* (published by Kogan Page), which summarises ten years' work in recognising, understanding and supporting entrepreneurs.

And, of course, obey the fundamental laws of entrepreneurship summarised in this toolkit.

Step 2: Invite entrepreneurs to talk

Invite entrepreneurs into your business to give inspiring talks to your people. Ask those from outside your industry to share their entrepreneurial experiences with your own staff.

Example

> Scottish Enterprise encouraged entrepreneurs to visit universities and colleges to tell their stories. Students then started asking their tutors to bring in people who could help them with venture capital, protecting intellectual property rights (IPR), finding premises and so on. In other words, this created 'demand pull' as opposed to trying to 'teach people' how to become entrepreneurs.

TIP: Ask people with recent business start-up experience to present their experiences. Theirs will be much closer to the realities of innovation and 'intrepreneurship' than big business leaders.

Step 3: Find the energy in your business

Entrepreneurship requires vision, passion and obsessive commitment, so find the people who have these qualities in your business and give them voice and support.

Ask people with ideas to come forward from whatever level or department. Give them the opportunity to pursue their ideas in your business – rather than see 50 per cent of them learn to start their own business at your expense!

Listen to new voices, too. Encourage diversity in your business thinking by listening to young people, customer-interfacing people and others who may not always spring immediately to mind.

Step 4: Let people try their ideas

Make it easy for people to start a business in *your* business. Give them space to experiment and try out their ideas.

An insurance company in Glasgow transformed a large old office into small units with screens, telephones and a computer. Anybody with an idea could spend half a day a week in that facility to experiment with their idea.

If the idea looked promising they could spend a day a week, then if it got even more promising they could spend all week in the new incubator. If the idea took off the company would share the equity with the employee.

Currently, eighteen new product ideas are being developed to launch stage.

Step 5: Bring Silicon Valley into your business

Silicon Valley has been described as the entrepreneurial capital of the world. What lessons can be learned from this centre of entrepreneurship? Silicon Valley works because it's a free market for:

- Talent – they don't care if you don't wear a pinstriped suit or didn't go to Oxford University.
- Ideas – they value good ideas from wherever they come.
- Capital – they try to make it easy for people to get capital.

This free market recipe generates thousands of new opportunities every year. So how can you create the same kind of entrepreneurial culture within your business?

Here are some ways that UK entrepreneurs have responded to this challenge:

- One UK blue-chip has taken 10 per cent out of its subsidiary companies' budgets in order to create a venture fund internally for innovation. Funds are now available for new business ideas.
- One brewery asked their 25-year-old smart graduate to come up with a new wine bar concept. They came up with the award-winning 'All Bar One' concept.
- A food manufacturer set up a company innovation team consisting of people they wanted to prepare for bigger roles. They gave them the space to identify and work on projects that would improve the business.

Step 6: Avoid blockages

Do not put bureaucratic blockages, even inadvertently, in the way of your fledgling 'intrepreneurs'. Basically, don't repeat the mistakes of the past (reread the section 'How *not* to create an "intrepreneurial" culture' above).

Listen to your 'intrepreneurs' and take any blockages out of their way that may be dissipating their energy and passion – the type of blockage that says, 'IT can't give us support until 2004'!

Step 7: Be prepared for some failures

If you are being entrepreneurial then you must expect some ideas to fail. You will be smart enough to ensure you do not bet your business on a deal too easily!

As one MD said, 'If we don't get a few no-shows, then we're not taking enough risks.'

Step 8: Encourage persistence
Innovation takes time, so encourage people to keep going. It took James Dyson 587 goes to perfect his world-breaking Dyson cleaner.

Step 9: Keep the process informal
Do not try to formalise the innovation process, but allow it to germinate and grow. Entrepreneurship is an informal, idiosyncratic, often trial-and-error process. You need to try to keep this informality for as long as possible.

Step 10: Learn from successful peers
Keep an eye on what other 'intrepreneurial' businesses are doing. There are a number of different approaches being tried and developed right now including:

- incubators inside and outside companies
- clusters of business
- start-ups within a business
- internal venture funds

We are keeping an eye on what's happening worldwide and will report any new good ideas or developments on our website, www.davidhalluk.com.

Toolkit 24: Developing a superior product or service

- Gain a larger share of your customers' business.
- Create new winning products or service.
- Get new products to market more effectively.

One of the key ways of building stronger partnerships with customers and staying ahead of the competition is to invest in new products and services. A survey by London Business School found that 62 per cent of businesses believe that the intensity of competition is the principal external barrier to growth. This was caused primarily by a narrow product market focus. Creating new products and services, therefore, is a key way to break out of the competitive spiral.

The most effective way to gain competitive advantage and higher prices is to design and develop superior products and services. As one CEO elegantly put it, 'You can't market rubbish.' Businesses often have to overspend on marketing and selling their products when they are just the same as their competitors. 'We are no worse than anyone else,' is how another MD described their mediocre product offering. The best way to build a business is to develop a superior product or service.

Story –Triple 'A' Ranch

What do you normally get when you book your favourite pet into a kennel while you go on holiday? Your pet gets looked after with an occasional walk, and when you return it is delighted to see you. Not at the Triple 'A' Ranch.

When you book your pet in they ask for your pet's favourite TV shows so that they can video them for the animal while you are away.

Your pet can have up to five walks a day with someone who is a real pet lover. Extras include aerobics for dogs and sports for cats. You can telephone and talk to your pet direct via the portable telephone system. Your pet is so well looked after that when you return it does not want to come with you! But it does not end there. When you arrive home there is a postcard from your pet saying what a great time it had and asking when you are going on holiday again.

Ann Adlington and her team at Triple 'A' Ranch have transformed commodity-type dog-kennel businesses into a five-star pet-care service.

Her reward is that she charges twice as much as her competitors with a high level of repeat business and referrals.

FOOTNOTE: Ann Adlington sold her business for a substantial profit to an American business in 2000.

Here's how to do it:

Step 1: Create a vision

Your vision needs to include becoming the industry leader. Create an exciting vision, which does not include compromising quality at any cost. Consider using Toolkit 8, 'Creating a vision for your business'.

Step 2: Get some new values and change your internal drivers

- attention to minute detail
- uncompromising quality
- pushing back all the boundaries
- being the best you possibly can be
- getting the best ideas from outside the industry
- constantly innovating
- taking responsibility for lifting the performance of the whole industry
- daring to be different
- and more ...

Step 3: Look for opportunities

Be on the lookout for opportunities to improve your product. Examine your product from every angle. Ask yourself whether you can make it smaller, lighter, easier.

As how you could improve its performance, and what boundaries you should be pushing back. For instance:

- technology
- design
- utility
- simplicity
- ease of use

Could you work in partnership with a university research group in order to research and develop the product? If you held a focus group of customers and asked them what improvements they would like to see, what would they tell you?

How can you leverage your brand promise by developing complementary products? What about the labelling and packaging? Can you make it simpler to read, and not use:

- self-assembly furniture with 500 pieces and the instructions in Arabic?
- shrink-wrap that is virtually impossible to remove?

Step 4: Get outside the box

Look outside your industry for state-of-the-art new ideas or good practice.

Example

> A construction group thought they were buying well. They then asked the question, 'Who buys well?' The answer was that retailers buy well. But which retailer? Wal-Mart. So they brought Wal-Mart in to describe how they buy. The construction group found ways to take 9 per cent out of their purchases over a twelve-month period, which put 50 per cent on to the group's profits.

Why not book yourself a trip to California to see what's happening there? Or try holding off-the-wall brainstorming sessions with your team.

Monitor social trends and changes. For example, people's preference for eating out more has led to an annual 25 per cent growth in the demand for sandwich bars.

Step 5: Force-fit things together

The Yo Sushi chain was developed as a unique product by combining sushi eating (a growing trend) with robots from factories. This created a new dining experience where robots act as waiters and even cook rice. Nothing had been seen like it before.

One business combined sports and pets, which created a new product. They now supply all the UK premier football league clubs with dog leads and eating bowls in the club colours for sale in their own retail outlets.

Snack Apple in Australia combined sweets and apples to create a new product that children would eat. They cut apples into sections, covered them with a sweet (not sugar) coloured coating that tasted really good and looked attractive.

Brainstorm what you could force-fit your product with, in order to develop a new winning product.

Step 6: Develop prototypes for testing

Turn your best ideas into some low-cost prototypes in order to get some early customer reaction. Be persistent. This is new to your customers as well as you.

The person who invented Post-it notes was initially faced with negative feedback ('What do we want yellow sticky bits of paper for?') Now it's a world-beating product.

So turn the best prototype into products, test them and monitor customer reaction. The acid test is that, if you really have developed a superior product or service, then you should enjoy these benefits:

- You can put your price up significantly higher than the competition.
- You will get opportunities from repeat business and word-of-mouth recommendations.
- You will not have to promote your product using expensive marketing and sales methods.

If you do not enjoy these benefits then it's back to Step 1, I'm afraid.

Step 7: Continuous development

Your competitors won't stand still, so you need to create a culture in which everybody is encouraged to contribute ideas on how to improve any detail of the product.

For instance, the female dog handlers at Triple 'A' Ranch contributed most of the ideas that made the business the best in the industry over a ten-year period.

Continuous improvement should, like a pet, be for life, not just for Christmas.

Twelve key lessons

Here are twelve new product development (NPD) lessons from successful businesspeople.

1. The success rate of NPD can be greatly enhanced if it is part of the strategic development of the business and particularly of the building of long-term partnerships with customers.

For example, the construction industry has been challenged to improve its partnership and supply-chain management by the Egan report. (This 1998 report, set up by the government, reviewed construction industry practice and made recommendations about developing supply chain management.) Some large companies are using this opportunity to develop partnerships with joint NPD projects with their customers.

2. Leaders of NPD need to understand the difference between an idea (something we are obsessed with) and an opportunity (something that meets our customer needs).

For example, Clive Sinclair was obsessed with his C5 car – the customers hated it.

3. NPD should be a commercially led activity.

For example, 3M Innovation described their definition of innovation as the commercialisation of new ideas.

4. Get very early input from the target customer on the product concept.

Northern Foods PLC developed a new concept that included differently coloured packaging for different products. Early customer focus groups suggested that they wanted one-colour, simple packaging. 'This was the breakthrough that allowed the product to be a success,' said the NPD commercial manager.

5. Learn to listen well to customers right from the concept stage.

Problems with internal experts are that, *because* they are experts, they often have too big an ego to listen to people both internally and externally. E.g., '90 per cent of business problems would disappear if they only learned to talk to each other more internally and listen to customers externally,' write O'Shea and Madigan in their book, *Dangerous Company.*

6. Create a culture internally where anybody feels able to suggest ideas for new products regardless of their job role or status.

For example, Silicon Valley works because it has created a free open market for talent, ideas and capital. Silicon Valley companies care less about status or rank than they do about the quality of the product ideas. How many new product ideas do you get from your people?

7. Get focus into your NPD.

Companies that have developed their NPD process often report that initially they went for quantity: lots of ideas at the concept stage, few of which turned into winners. This can be very expensive. They then move into a much more selective stage with a much higher rate of success.

8. Get really close to the commercial user of your product.

Many companies who sell through intermediaries such as retailers or distributors have found significant benefits by getting closer to their customer's customer. Many food manufacturers are going directly to consumers in order to identify new opportunities, and then working with the retailers in order to develop the products.

9. Make the process market-led, not production-driven.

There is a significant difference, for example, between the drivers of entrepreneurship in the UK and Australia. The Aussies, I found, were much more likely to search out opportunities and then worry about the resources to take up the opportunity later. In the UK, businesses often start with their existing capacity and look for ways to use it. 'Sweat the assets', as the CEO of a railway business described it.

The consequence is that NPD is a marginal process refining existing products rather than creating new ones. This narrows the product/market focus and intensifies competition.

10. Be persistent.

NPD is a creative process, often involving science, intuition, analysis, good marketing skills and creativity, but probably most importantly hard work.

'It took me 587 attempts to develop the Dyson Cleaner,' said James Dyson. Now that's persistence!

11. Set objectives for innovation.

3M Innovation's objective is that 25 per cent of all sales should come from products launched within the last four years.

12. Encourage skunkworking.

Skunkworking is doing things around the fringe of the business – not mainstream. Entrepreneurial NPD process often involves a passionate individual who spots an opportunity and won't let go of it.

CHAPTER EIGHT

Building Your Culture

 ## Toolkits 25–27

Toolkit 25: Using the EntreNet to really boost your business
Toolkit 26: Making work fun and enjoyable
Toolkit 27: Creating a preferred culture

 ## Toolkit 25: Using the EntreNet to really boost your business

- Share the wisdom within your business in order to boost its performance.
- Build your business's managerial capacity.
- Be consultants to yourselves.

A key proposition in this book is that most of the wisdom to make businesses work effectively resides within. However, it has proved very helpful to provide a process to help managers to mine the internal wisdom in order to create the business benefits. An opportunity exists for top management to pull the wisdom together from one team or project and spread it right across the business, 'After all,' you might say, 'we've paid for that learning once. Let's get the benefit *throughout* the business.'

This is the role for the EntreNet, which is a group of managers who create an internal network in order to share their wisdom around the business. I originally developed the EntreNet as a process to help entrepreneurs to learn from each other.

The entrepreneurial process they created was:

- spotting opportunities (to improve the business)
- marshalling the resources (to take up the opportunities)
- building the capability (to develop the opportunities)

Larger businesses realised that this creative problem-solving process could be very helpful in helping them entrepreneurially, sharing their internal wisdom. It has worked very effectively.

Story – DHP Enterprise

DHP Enterprise, a provider of training to start-up businesses for government-funded schemes, found that in Doncaster in South Yorkshire they could significantly boost the recruitment of trainees (unemployed people wanting to start their own business) by locating an adviser actually in a job centre to talk to people direct.

This tactic significantly boosted trainee numbers and exceeded their targets and income.

DHP Enterprise's managers in other offices also faced the same recruitment challenges, but it was not until a managers' meeting was held, where internal problems and solutions were discussed, that the Doncaster experience was shared for the benefits of the business overall.

The tactic was then rolled out to DHP's ten other offices across the country and produced results beyond expectations. This is a classic example of the multiplier effect of the EntreNet – spreading solutions right across a business.

There are a number of benefits of the EntreNet:

- The business has paid for the learning once; the EntreNet actually multiplies your return on that investment. 3M Innovation create internal EntreNets by sharing and learning technology right across the business and around the globe. They have found sharing provides competitive advantage and a basis for new product development.
- It's much cheaper being consultants to yourselves than hiring external 'experts'. People buy into solving their own problems.
- It creates a continuous improvement and development culture.

- It develops the managerial capacity within your business. Redland PLC's mission statement was 'to use our global skills in local markets'. They shared their internal wisdom around the globe. For example, they made bricks 20 per cent cheaper in their Australian business than in the UK, so they brought across their Australian team to help the UK business to cut costs.
- It helps people to learn how to solve problems.

So why isn't the EntreNet a natural process in every business, as it appears to be such an obvious idea? It often happens in business that common sense becomes rare sense, not because of business logic but for two main reasons.

One is that there is usually no process for sharing problems and solutions ('I have a problem with X; how can I find out who else has sorted this out in our business?').

The other concerns 'shadow-side' issues. The shadow side of the business is all those things that do not get discussed in formal meetings but *do* get talked about in pubs, corridors and canteens – in the shadows.

The shadow-side blockages to the EntreNet are:

- egos and unhealthy internal competition rather than collaboration
- the notion that it was 'not invented here so it can't be any good'
- turf wars – in some businesses there seems to be more competition internally than there is with the competitors
- career competition – 'This will make them look good if we adopt it'
- the idea that 'we do that already' – a blind belief that it's happening even when it isn't

Clearly what is needed is a process to identify and spread the internal wisdom across the business.

Here is how to do it:

Step 1: Call a representatives' meeting

Gather representatives – one from each business unit or department – together. If your business consists of business units spread geographically, get the general managers together. You can also organise a functional group of people to meet: for example, all the sales team or the production managers from each unit. You need to determine what is going to add most value to your business right now.

The aim of the meeting is to set up the EntreNet group. The meeting will normally take two to three hours.

Tell your managers that the purpose of the group is to be 'consultants to ourselves'. You want to share your internal wisdom for the benefit of the business overall. The sharing process is a two-way street. An individual may have a solution to an issue this time but may be the recipient of a solution next time.

Tell them you want people to collaborate and not compete, and you will not stand for any game playing or withholding of help, for whatever reason.

Try to have prepared a live example of success. For example, 'Fred sorted out the quality problem and shared it with three other units for the benefit of us all, which is what we want to encourage more of in our business.'

Get people to discuss any concerns they may have and deal with them upfront: 'I'm too busy' or 'We thought of it – why should we share it?'

Step 2: Kick off the process

Ask each individual to think about successes they have enjoyed in their business. This might include projects successfully completed, initiatives seized, improvements made, major problems solved or opportunities taken.

In order to help them identify success ask them:

- What has given the most pleasure?
- What are they really proud of?
- Where have they produced a result beyond expectations?

Ask them to identify successes that they are prepared to share or offer to their colleagues. Write these on a flipchart with their names alongside. Try to get each person to identify three as a minimum. These are the *offers*.

Ask them to try to put cost/benefits on the offers: for example, 'Making a resource available in the job centres doubled our sales in 1994.'

You may, as the boss, want to throw in some of your observations on their successes and needs from your perspective: for instance, 'I thought the way you resolved that purchasing problem, John, was a lesson to us all. Don't you want to include that in your successes?'

Now ask each individual to think about any current problems or challenges they face. This might be a new project, a complex problem, a political issue.

In order to help them identify their *needs*, ask them:

> ■ What might stop you achieving your plans this year?
> ■ What difficult problems do you face?
> ■ What new challenges have you taken on?
> ■ If you could resolve any issues right now that might move your business forward what might that be?
> ■ What, if anything, keeps you awake at night?

Ask individuals to write their needs on a flipchart with their name alongside. Aim for a minimum of three needs.

Ask individuals to put a cost-benefit estimate to each need, such as 'need to improve delivery performance'. The benefit could be an additional £100k profit this year. This helps to prioritise the needs.

Step 3: Share needs and offers
Ask each individual to present quickly, in one/two sentences, their needs and offers to the rest of the group. Match any obvious needs and offers: for example, 'Mick needs to cut overheads; Anne has been highly successful in cutting costs. You should talk to each other.' Anne will spend some time sharing her wisdom with Mick on how she achieved the result.

Once the obvious matchings have taken place, ask individuals who have either not had a need met or not had an offer taken up to select a need they are prepared to help with and a need they have that they would like somebody to help them with.

The objective is for everybody by the end of the meeting to have a plan to get at least one need met and get one of their offers taken up.

Step 4: Establish the next steps
The task for each individual is:

a. To work on their need. Clearly in practice they may delegate this to a member of their team. It matters less who does it but that it gets done.

b. Provide their offers of help to one other person. Again they may delegate this to somebody more appropriate in their team.

Arrange a review meeting in say six weeks' or two months' time to review progress. At the review meeting individuals will share progress and lessons learned with each other.

> TIP: A key blockage to progress is often the need to make internal people and resources available to work on initiatives. The boss's job is to help them focus and help identify resources. Remember the potential payoffs from the multiplier.

Step 5: The first review meeting

Make this upbeat and energetic. Ask individuals to prepare a short presentation of what they have been doing, their achievements and future intention with their identified tasks. Celebrate success and share lessons.

If people have met obstacles or problems, discuss as a group how they might help resolve them.

There may be projects that can be rolled out right across the business in order to get the real benefits of the multiplier. Discuss how you might do this as a business. Make resources available to do it well.

At the end of the meeting review any general lessons about improving your business. Keep a record of the projects undertaken and the potential benefits to the business overall.

Step 6: Continue the process

Go back to Step 2 and repeat the process on an ongoing basis.

Step 7: Repeat step 6 ...

> Tip: Consider putting all your company projects on to a database that anyone can access. This could be one-page objectives, processes, outcomes, learning points and contact person. Many large companies have hundreds of projects and initiatives often with overlap between them. Capturing the organisation's corporate memory and wisdom really is a powerful sharing process.

Summary

Put cost benefits to each need and offer. This process helps prioritise and allocate the appropriate resource.

Encourage project leaders to make internal resources available. One of the big insights into why organisations often fail to change and adapt is that, although they spot the opportunities, they do not allocate the people resources to take up the opportunities. Therefore, they are unable to build the capability within to take up the opportunities.

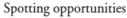

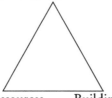

Spotting opportunities

Marshalling resources   Building capability

Be persistent. Keep going.

Encourage collaboration, banish competition.

The EntreNet is often countercultural within businesses used to a profit-centred, management-competitive culture. You really do need to convince them of the benefits.

Toolkit 26: Making work fun and enjoyable

- Increase motivation, commitment and creativity.
- Achieve a better work/life balance.
- Put a smile on people's faces at work.

'All work and no play makes Jack a dull boy,' goes the old adage. There seems to be a correlation between businesses in which people enjoy what they do and a high level of productivity, creativity, commitment and even willingness to change.

Story – Northern Foods PLC

Mike Morgan, personnel director of Northern Foods, cherished what he believed to be one of his business's key values. 'Let's not take ourselves too seriously,' he said. 'It's hard to pin down our culture, but it's something about asking questions in all directions and working hard at listening to people. We want to have a bit of fun, too.'

It was unsurprising, then, that the management consultant

> Professor Gerard Egan described the Northern Foods people culture as one of the healthiest he had seen.

Why is making work enjoyable in business important today? Why does it seem to make good business sense? Here are some observations from recent studies:

- Stress in the workplace has never been higher.
- People are more affluent today, yet there are more depressed people than ever.
- People are working longer hours and in many areas much harder.
- There is increasing competition rather than collaboration between people at work.
- A high percentage of people report that they do not enjoy their work any more.
- Many large companies are downsizing and changing structures, creating uncertainty.
- In many cases people have lost faith in leaders. Note the record low turnout in the 2001 UK general election.

Consequently some businesses have to pay well over the odds, in some cases having to bribe their staff to stay with them.

We businesspeople have a responsibility to restore some fun and sanity in people's lives. It can also make good business sense.

Example

> Dr Peter Honey, a management trainer, found that when he was running ideas-generation workshops for American Express the quality and quantity of ideas increased significantly in those groups that were laughing, joking and generally having a good time.

Having fun engages the right hemisphere of the brain, which unleashes creativity, innovation, intuition and entrepreneurial thinking. You don't get the impression there is much right-brain working going on in some of the turgid management meetings that I occasionally have to suffer.

I once visited a UK clearing bank, who told me they wanted to increase innovation and creativity and make work more fun. Perhaps typically, as a left-brain, rational-thinking institution, they initiated 'the happy half-hour' between 9.30 and 10 a.m. every Wednesday.

People were made to put up balloons and streamers, take off their ties, wear silly hats and loosen up.

In all honestly, I felt embarrassed for them: they looked extremely uncomfortable and couldn't wait for the half-hour to end. This kind of 'planned spontaneity' rarely seems to work in practice. So what does work?

Get your team together and tell them that fun is compulsory and anyone who is not constantly telling jokes will be sacked ... Only joking – but I hope it put a smile on your face.

Story – Keepmoat PLC

> Keepmoat are a construction group who regularly entertain customers at their box at the Doncaster racecourse. They also hold golf days for customers. However, they also use their entertaining facilities to entertain their staff at all levels, including labourers and bricklayers as well as management. Everybody gets treated with respect and exactly the same, regardless of rank. Everybody has a great time and it is very much appreciated by all concerned.
>
> Guess who are the market leaders and the most profitable business in their sector ...

It's a bit difficult to produce a sequential step-by-step guide to fun but here are some steps you can take to make the workplace more enjoyable for everyone.

Step 1: Get fun into your vision

Include fun and enjoying work in your vision and values. Learn from Mike Morgan at Northern Foods: 'Let's not take ourselves too seriously.'

Balance the stakeholder benefits in your vision and values, and include your people values. For example, make your company an enjoyable place to work; indeed, make it a culture where people *want to come* to work.

The MD of Redland Brick told me his vision was that his people come to work happy. I asked what he meant. He told me to look out of the window. It was 8.45 a.m. and people were coming into work looking as if they were attending a funeral. I didn't think they would be killing for Redland that day ...

Make yours a business that encourages people to become the best they can be, as well as being a friendly place to work.

Step 2: Be a 'fun' role model

Make time to have a laugh and a joke with people. Ensure you treat everyone the same – as you wish people to treat you.

And feel able to laugh at yourself sometimes. Keepmoat PLC held a charity day with all staff. The chairman, Terry Bramall, put himself in the stocks so that people could throw wet sponges at him.

Make somebody's day. Do something special for somebody. It could be giving a very special award for twenty years' service.

Step 3: Try to lighten meetings and events

Make sure you have a laugh and a joke during management meetings. Keep meetings as short as possible by imposing an end time as well as a start time.

Change the venue for meetings. Meet in a hotel, for instance, and arrange lunch afterwards. This changes the rhythm and people enjoy it.

Step 4: Smarten up the workplace

Tidy up the public areas at work.

Example

> An advertising agency in London recognised that they were in the knowledge-sharing business internally in order to create opportunities. So they refurbished the staff dining area. Out went the plastic chairs, cold lino and faulty coffee machines and it became a five-star facility. This included leather settees, a TV and good free refreshment facilities.
>
> They found that their staff really appreciated these new facilities and used the area to meet, share ideas and be more creative.

Make sure the staff facilities are up to five-star standards, and ensure people have really comfortable chairs to sit on all day.

Example

The Hilton 2000 conference centre has invested in 24-hour comfortable swivel conference chairs. After 10 hours you still feel really fresh. I personally don't want to go to any other conference facility any more.

Step 5: Hold fun events

Take people out for a beer after work, ban talking about work and have some fun. Take staff to the races or to play golf, perhaps with a customer's staff. You get the double benefit of networking and having fun.

Dare to be creative. Do something different from the boring Christmas party. Steetley PLC took their people on the *Orient Express* for Christmas dinner. Staff talked about the brilliant time they had for years afterwards.

Step 6: Remove the bureaucracy

It has been estimated that 40–70 per cent of white-collar workers' efforts add no value. Increasingly, people are asked to attend more meetings, deal with more paperwork and handle a plethora of emails daily.

How can you reduce some of this burden and make work much more fun and be more productive? One idea is to have a paperwork audit carried out in the office and reduce some of the paperwork. One architectural business found that they were filling in contract values on 27 different documents. Companies find that they can reduce the paperwork by at least 50 per cent with no negative impact on the business.

Get the e-mail system reviewed. Some managers are spending up to an hour and a half a day reviewing hundreds of internal emails, most of which are rubbish. If you multiply this by the number of managers, the cost is into millions of pounds wasted. A food manufacturer installed some simple guidelines on the use of internal emails. This included banning the use of 'copy-to-all' internal emails, which were reduced from an average of 150 to 10 per day, releasing up to one hour's time per person.

Reduce reportage and planning bureaucracy. A builder reduced the business planning process from a fifty-page document to just three pages. This had the additional benefit of allowing the managers to focus on the really important strategic priorities in the plan.

Step 7: Make change an adventure, not a trauma

The blockages to change and growth in business are:

> ■ That top management believe and act as if everybody in the business needed to change but them.
>
> **Action**: Act as a role model for change. Make sure you show your personal commitment to doing things differently.

- That there is no process to encourage people to change.

  Action: Use the toolkits in this book to involve your people in the change plan.

- That resistance to change is created when the command-and-control culture is used to try to force change through the business.

  Action: Engage people in the change process. Work with the people who have energy and commitment. Get some quick wins. Use the Toolkit 7, 'Working on the business'.

Step 8: Look after yourself

Make sure you keep a balance between work and having fun in order to recharge your batteries. You can't be a fun role model if you are a workaholic.

Example

> When I worked at Steetley PLC, the MD used to come to work every morning looking as if he had the trouble of the world on his shoulders, grunting at people. Staff would ask me, 'Are we going bust? Is the share price about to dive?' They were genuinely concerned by what they read into his body language.
>
> Eventually I persuaded the MD to come to work wearing a smile and, no matter how he felt, to say good morning pleasantly. People then stopped asking the worried questions.

Make time to play sport, take decent holidays or take up invitations to the races. You can always justify it to yourself if you have to: it's 'networking'.

If you have become a workaholic (as I did) and you have given up on your hobbies and interests, think about the things that you used to enjoy when you were younger. My brother used to love cycling and playing cricket in his youth. Recently, at fifty, he purchased a bike and started playing cricket again in his son's Sunday team. He is like a new man.

Toolkit 27: Creating a preferred culture

- Design a culture that serves your business.
- Develop consistency in 'the way we do things here'.
- Make your culture an asset rather than a liability.

Culture is the way we do things here. Strategy is *what* we intend to do; culture is *how* we will achieve it. Inevitably culture lags behind strategy, so a key management task is to ensure that a culture is developed that supports the strategy.

Story – EWS Railway Limited

This UK rail freight business was born after British Rail went through several owners to end up as EWS.

It had bits of several organisation cultures, including the best and worst of the old British Rail business. The new CEO, Philip Mengel, decided that he wanted an EWS culture that served the needs of the new business. His team developed some values that would underpin the way things got done, including:

- trust
- measurement
- continuous improvement
- a policy of 'customer first'
- passion

These values described the new EWS way of doing business. An internal team set out to identify where the business behaved in line with the values and where the values were contravened. People's views were sought from around the business. This led to a major initiative of putting customers first, which significantly boosted customer satisfaction ratings. The team found lots of passion in the business – indeed, they discovered that this value was already part of the prevailing culture. 'Rules' and practices that contravened the trust value were rescinded.

The second stage was to start to measure things and to establish key indicators leading to a programme of continuous improvement. EWS is in a much better shape in 2001 than it was when Philip Mengel took over and it looks to have a bright future.

It's a good example of culture driving change in a complex business.

All businesses have a culture. The key issue is to have the culture you want or prefer, otherwise you will get a culture by default – one that could well hold the business back.

A construction-materials group MD once told me, 'Our strategy is to compete by delivering consistent high standards of customer service. Yet our traditional reactive, production-driven culture means we are unable to achieve our desired service levels. Our culture was once described as "we will let you have what we decide, when we decide, at a price we decide".'

This really meant that the service strategy was undoable. So culture can be an asset if it serves your business or a liability if it holds you back.

This toolkit has been designed to help you design and develop a culture that really does serve your business. But first let's get to grips with what culture is all about. Culture is a set of shared beliefs about how we should do business. For instance, we might say we believe we must deliver on time – whatever it takes.

This leads to a set of values, which are not usually compromised – delighting our customers, for example.

This then creates consistent shared behaviours in the business: everybody, including the receptionist, the drivers and the MD, sets out to delight customers. This is non-negotiable and becomes 'just the way we do things here'.

Here is how to create a preferred culture.

Step 1: Establish your preferred culture

First of all, call together the team and establish a preferred culture for your business. Decide what it is of which you can say, 'This is the way we want to do things around here.'

Get the team to brainstorm your core values (see the EWS story above). You really need only six or seven core values, which should describe how you want to do business internally and externally and are critical to the success for the delivery of your strategy. Typical values could be to:

- delight our customers
- stick to the products we know
- treat each other with respect
- be ethical in all we do
- present no surprises to shareholders
- collaborate rather than compete

Step 2: Communicate your preferred culture internally

Tell people about your values at every opportunity.

> TIP: Make sure you personally behave in line with the values.

Include the values in your key documents: strategy, business plans, presentations to key stakeholders. Explain what the values mean using live examples from your business. For example:

- 'We value putting our customers first. This means everybody pulls out all the stops to serve customers.'
- 'In order to do that we will staff the sales desk from 8 a.m. through to 6 p.m. rather than 9 a.m. to 5 p.m.'
- 'We will agree and monitor service standards with our customers.'
- 'Top managers will visit our key customers monthly.'

Story – Keepmoat PLC

Keepmoat PLC decided in 1990 that delighting customers needed to be a core value. They wanted to develop a customer-orientated culture.

Initially, their staff were very sceptical: 'Delighting customers in construction? You must be joking!'

However, the management persisted and talked consistently about delighting customers. They appointed customer liaison managers on their building sites. They measured customer delight monthly through surveys. They trained people and made delighting customers a non-negotiable part of their way of doing business.

As a result, ten years on, they were negotiating much more of their work with their customers (much more profitable than tendering). They are the preferred suppliers for many local authorities and housing associations.

'Delighting customers is now our competitive advantage. Yet it took us quite a while to build into the way we do business,' says Dick Watson, the CEO of Keepmoat PLC.

A good example of culture as a real asset.

> TIP: Values need to be translated into action by taking positive steps to *live* them or make them drive business behaviour. People become cynical about values when they don't see the organisation doing anything to live up to them.

Step 3: Get the culture owned in business groups

This means cascading the values throughout the business by allowing departments and teams to determine what the values mean for them. It also means allowing them to put their 'smell' on the values.

A powerful way of achieving this is to get your team leaders to work with their teams on deciding exactly what the values mean for them. For example, if you had a value 'measurement', then when this is cascaded by, say, the HR team: 'This means we need to measure labour turnover, percentage of training plans implemented, staff satisfaction levels, productivity levels ...'

Step 4: Build your new culture into your business

Establish rituals that reinforce the culture. For example, if being innovative is a value then put innovation as a regular item on team agendas; or, if performance beyond the norm is a value, then make sure you have weekly or monthly public performance awards for people who produce outstanding results.

Tell stories that reinforce your culture. Chris O'Reilly, the owner of LDM, the document specialists, tells the story of his longest stint at a photocopier: forty hours without a break. This reinforces the value of hard work and commitment.

Ensure your systems support your culture. Keepmoat have a system of monitoring customer delight on a weekly basis because it is a key value in their business.

You should also act as a role model for your culture. If one of your values is continuous improvement, make sure you *visibly* continuously improve the things you do.

Step 5: Identify blockages

Working with your team, seek to identify any blockages in developing your preferred culture. These will probably include:

1. Covert norms

These are leftovers from the old culture: 'We always did it this way ...' or 'We traditionally promote people using the civil service principle of length of service, not performance ...'

Covert norms need to be challenged and changed by establishing new rules, routines and agreements.

2. Internal politics

This shows up as game playing and shadow-side issues between departments or individuals: 'Sales don't really talk to production: they actually hate each other…' or 'Profit centre managers think HQ is a waste of money so they do their own thing and ignore head office initiatives.'

The politics of self-interest, which are not in line with the new value, need to be challenged and banished.

3. Key holdouts

Some people refuse to imbibe the new values. They are wedded to the old ways of doing things.

You really need to work on these people in order to get them to change. If they cannot and they are a major problem or threat to the business, you need to decide whether one individual is bigger or more important than the business.

In practice, removing blockages to cultural change is often one of the most difficult tasks managers face in businesses today. Stick at it – the prize is worth it.

Step 6: Set up culture review processes

This means ensuring there are rewards for implementing the new values and consequences for ignoring them.

As my friend Gerard Egan says, 'If you want to change culture, change the reward system.' So what do the culture champions in your business get for imbibing the new culture? And what happens to those dinosaurs who are unwilling to change?

Finally, integrate the new values into your existing processes. Make them part of the induction process. Include them in your business plans. Review the use of the values in your performance management system or appraisal process.

CHAPTER NINE

Become More Efficient and Effective

Toolkits 28–29

Toolkit 28: Fixing system slippage
Toolkit 29: Removing process blocks and disconnects

Toolkit 28: Fixing system slippage

 Boost profits, customer service and the efficiency of your business.

 Create an internal war chest for reinvesting in your business.

 Renew the entrepreneurial spirit and energy within your business.

System slippage is the gap between systems, rules or guidelines that businesses establish and their lack of consistent use in practice. Fixing it is a very effective way to get significant improvements in performance and profit.

For instance, your policy may that all customer complaints be logged and dealt with within 24 hours – but in practice only certain diligent people comply with this rule.

Businesses are not as effective as they might be if the rules or systems were used consistently. So you could get customers saying, 'They don't care about us; they don't treat us seriously when we complain,' or 'We will take our business elsewhere next time.'

Fixing any system slippages provides the opportunity to revitalise the business by boosting profits, service levels and efficiency. In practice many businesses have been surprised to find that they are haemorrhaging costs with the slippages often equating to at least the annual net profits of the business.

'Fixing system slippage helped us to quadruple our profits in one year,' says Simon Keats, MD of North Staffs Caravans. 'It also got us out of the doldrums and going again.'

> TIP: The easiest way to make money is to stop losing it.

Why does system slippage occur?
Here are some of the main reasons why the system slips:

- 'We never properly monitored or audited our credit-control system.'
- 'Our new recruits were not trained to use our system.'
- Different people have their 'own unique way' of doing things.
- 'We [the management] believed the system was being used when it wasn't.'
- There are no apparent consequences of using or not using the system.
- There are inevitable gaps between policy and practice at the sharp end.

The benefits of fixing system slippage
In order to get your juices flowing, here are some of the financial gains of identifying and fixing system slippage:

	Value £
Not following the process for the selection of suppliers (suppliers inflated their quotations) – a building contractor.	410,000
Not following procedures for purchasing stationery – a consultancy business.	18,500
Not following the order entry process properly, causing major customer-service problems – a regional newspaper group.	Est. 1 million
Not completing risk management at commencement of a project (three projects went off track) – a civil engineering contractor.	760,000
Not taking up references for a senior appointment (candidate lied about experience and qualifications) – a bank.	21,000

	Value £
Not following process for 'cross-selling' extras to customers – a caravan retailer.	485,000
Not following established production planning system (resulting in conflict between sales and production) – a lintel manufacturer.	250,000

It is obvious that the benefits are worth having. Let's look at some examples in more detail.

Story – Countrywide Caravans

Brian Fairey, the owner of Countrywide Caravans, wanted to boost his profits. 'We have a £10 million business; we are working hard for nothing; we deserve to do better.'

Brian assembled his sales team from his four retail outlets, six people in total. Countrywide sold touring caravans, finance, insurance, servicing and spares through retail outlets. I and my colleagues took Brian's team through this toolkit. They identified that cross-selling was a key process, that is, encouraging the salespeople to sell all the Countrywide products as a total package, not just touring caravans.

The rationale was that the profit potential was in the extras, not in the sale of the caravan.

(This is a key point. Try to identify the real profit improvement opportunities in the business and focus upon them.)

I asked Brian Fairey what systems they had to ensure that the sales team offered the full package during every sale.

'We have a checklist for that,' said Brian, 'which is signed by every salesperson who makes a sale, and I see every form, so we don't have a problem.'

Brian left the meeting and I then asked the sales force bluntly: 'Do you all use this checklist?'

'Yes.'

'All the time?'

'Yes.'

'Look me in the eyes – do you use it all the time?'

'Well … John does.'

'What about the rest?'

'Well … some of the time …'

'What's some of the time?'

And out it came: 'We're here to sell caravans, not finance and spares ...'

It turned out they were not cross-selling all the additional services, but simply ticking the boxes on the sales form. A classic example of system slippage in living colour.

Why did the system not work? Three sales people were not trained in selling finance, nobody monitored the system in use and Brian never fully audited the system properly.

Brian retrained people and re-established the system, and profit went from £80k to £400k in three months.

'We now work smarter, not harder,' he said, 'and are actively looking at other areas of system slippage, which will boost our profits even further.'

This is a good example of the manager establishing a system and therefore believing he had everything under control.

BRIAN'S TIP: Inspect, don't expect, particularly those systems that hold real profit potential.

Story – A Regional Newspaper Group

'We've been trying for twelve months to reduce the mistakes we make in invoicing – it's really upsetting some of our customers,' said a frustrated Kim Armstrong, the financial controller. 'We can't identify and fix the problems. It's costing us £1.25 million per year.'

So a group of ten people from several departments and levels within the business were assembled. They were taken through the system slippage process and set off in small teams to try to identify the slippages in the process.

In order to understand the process fully, the team mapped the whole order entry system. This highlighted many issues and opportunities for improvements.

One team came back having found that 80 per cent of the problems were being caused by not attaching numbers to orders and so, when customers were invoiced, they could not trace the order, which is what brought about the disputes.

'Can't be right,' said Mark Pennistone, the operations director. 'Our policy is no order number, no order – simple. You must have made a mistake!'

'Excuse me,' piped up a young telephone sales trainee. 'I've just attended the sales training course and they teach you to get the order and worry about the paperwork later.'

This was a classic example of the difference between policy and practice in a large organisation. It reinforces the need to see the problems from several different perspectives within the business.

Everyone fell silent and Mark Pennistone's jaw dropped. The company were actually teaching their staff to ignore their own policy!

It was also discovered that it was not just the outstanding debt of £1.25 million that was the problem. They were taking their key customers to court and had seven admin people chasing outstanding debts.

The old rule that had slipped was reinstated, the training course changed and the computer software rewritten so as not to allow orders to be processed without the correct order number. Orders were also confirmed by fax to minimise disputes. The new process map was introduced and people were trained in the new process.

'It took us six months to sort out our customer disputes. They dropped from 700 to 27 per month and our debtors from £1.25 million to £130k. Fixing the system slippage added £1 million straight into our cash flow, improved our customer relations and released seven admin staff to work on more added-value work.'

The team's report to the board contained several benefits to the business:

- improved revenue/bottom-line profit
- retention of customer
- improved productivity
- removal of blame culture
- additional flexibility
- improved internal relationships

The next stage is to exceed customer expectations in line with the company vision.

KIM'S TIP: Involve people at the sharp end who know what's really happening in your business.

> TIP: Let your team read the stories in this toolkit in order to
> inspire them and to spark off their thinking about the
> opportunities in your business.

So how do you go about fixing system slippage? Follow these steps:

Step 1: Select your level of investigation

Select your level of investigation – decide whether the problem is
company-wide or just within a department.

> **Levels of system slippage**
> Whole business – often small businesses look at their business
> overall
> Department – e.g., production or sales
> Process flow – e.g., customer service or new product development
> Sub process – e.g., credit management as part of the customer
> service process
> High cost or problem areas

Select a cross section of your people to work as a team on fixing
system slippage.

> **Team selection hints**
> Have a maximum of ten people
> Choose people with different functions: e.g., sales or production
> Choose people of different levels: e.g., managers or operators
> Ensure users of the system are included
> Pick people who will contribute

Tell them you want to improve the profits, efficiency and service
levels in the business.

Say, 'We can either bring consultants in to do it or we can be consultants to ourselves – which do you want?' Most teams opt for the
latter choice! The first meeting should take half a day to a day.

Establish the ground rules with the team. Get them to come up
with the rules in order to get ownership.

> **Ground rules – an example**
> No finger pointing
> Treat each other with respect
> Be really honest
> Take the actions you agree to

Get the facts – no guessing
Adopt positive can-do attitudes
Make it fun and exciting – an adventure, not a trauma

Remember, well begun is half done.

Step 2: List the systems

Get the team to list the systems, processes and guidelines, both formal and informal, in place to control your business.

Checklist – typical system processes and guidelines
Level of system slippage – whole business

- recording the source of new customer enquiries
- recording customer details accurately
- terms and conditions communicated to customers
- customer expectations of you
- taking an order
- dealing with complaints
- controlling quality
- process for cross selling
- sales effectiveness
- productivity
- waste management
- cost control
- product profitability
- buying effectively
- obtaining customer feedback
- controlling costs
- recruiting people
- risk management processes
- marketing effectiveness
- database quality control

What are some of your key processes?

....
....
....
....
....

List the systems and processes that you use in your business on a flipchart. Do not reinterpret at this stage: record their words verbatim.

Step 3: Investigate the systems

Ask individuals to investigate which systems are being used effectively and consistently and which are not used or are used inconsistently. For instance, is there a system for recording sources of new enquiries, but in practice is not filled in adequately or in enough detail? (The consequence of this would be that there would be no way of assessing the effectiveness of your marketing – e.g., how new customers are created.)

They can have help from anybody in the business to do this. You should clear this with people.

If the system is complicated it may be helpful to map it as a process flowchart. This helps identify blockages, disconnects and problems. The newspaper group mapped their processes and found lots of gaps, so they remapped them as part of fixing the slippages.

Divide up the work among the team. Try to get them to work as singles or in pairs. Make sure you personally commit to an action – you are an important role model.

The brief is to investigate the system to see whether it is being used properly 100 per cent of the time. They need to be creative by asking people, sampling, watching and doing analysis of data where appropriate.

> TIP: Make sure you don't get people with vested interests evaluating themselves – for example, buyers looking at buying.

Agree a time frame – say, one month – to report back on the slippages to the systems.

> TIPS:
> - If the benefit is big enough consider making the project leader's role a full-time one.
> - Put your best people on to projects, not just those who are available.

Step 4: First review meeting

List slippages and causes on a flipchart, including those where further analysis might be required. Make sure you have completed your personal actions.

> TIPS:
>
> ■ Show interest between the meetings by asking people how they are doing investigating slippages. Inform them of your progress. Try to get momentum into the process.
>
> ■ Remove any blockages that people find – e.g., that the accounts department is too busy to provide information required. Remember, the prize is worth it.

Step 5: The financial consequences

Calculate the financial consequences of the slippages, such as not using the systems effectively. This creates a priority on the order in which you might deal with the slippages.

System slippage costs – an example	£000
Marketing spend	100
Buying effectiveness	200
Cost control process	50
Waste	12
Lack of planning	200
Cost of invoice disputes	120

So we are spending £100k on marketing, but if the recording system for new customers was used properly and consistently then we could reduce that to £10k, because we would know where new leads come from.

Step 6: Prioritise

Prioritise the systems you are going to reinstall by the cost-benefit analysis in Step 5. Keep this to an estimate on an annual basis: e.g.; waste costs £1k per month, which equates to £12k per annum.

> TIP: Keep the bean counters out of the process – this is a management job!

Step 7: Re-establish the system

Allocate individuals and teams to re-establish the system, train people in it, set up a monitoring process and make someone personally responsible for it on an ongoing basis.

If necessary reset new standards and produce a new process map.

Step 8: Review

Review and share progress on a regular basis until the job is completed.

Meet monthly as a whole team and report progress, lessons and problems to each other as the system slippages get fixed. Keep the momentum. Some can be done immediately, others, like the newspaper story, can take up to six or nine months. Celebrate success and share lessons around the business. Take the team out to dinner to celebrate!

> TIP: Keep going, be persistent. Success often comes just as you are about to give up!

Troubleshooter

Potential problems	Suggested remedies
People 'too busy' to attend meetings.	Work with those people who have the energy to change things or threaten with external consultants.
A command-and-control culture means people find it difficult to be open and honest.	Make sure you overdo agreeing the ground rules and the setting-up process right at the start. Spend time on this stage. Reinforce the ground rules by giving your personal pledge that you support the process.
Difficulty in tracing cause of slippage.	Consider mapping the process in detail. Keep asking why things happen. Get into the detail and probe until you find the cause.
People do not complete their actions.	Remind people of the ground rules. Act as a role model by completing your actions. Keep an 'action-ometer': i.e., calculate the percentage of actions completed on an ongoing basis and circulate to all team members weekly as a barometer of progress.

Toolkit 29: Removing process blocks and disconnects

■ Boost the efficiency and effectiveness of your business.

- Remove the 'silo syndrome'.
- Build cross-functional empathy and collaboration.

No business is just a collection of people. It is also a collection of processes, many of which may have never been really managed. In most businesses they just evolved over the years. Nobody took responsibility for designing them and nobody makes sure they perform as they should. Pick one – say, your customer service process. Check it out.

Chances are you will find no one person is in charge of the process. Lots of people have their fingerprints on it, but no single individual is accountable for the overall process results. Is this any way to run a business?

Story – Just Too Late!

A colleague was called in by a manufacturing company based in Sheffield to help them to improve their lead times. They were losing customers because they had a six-week lead time and their competitors could deliver in three weeks. Their deliveries were just too late.

My colleague calculated that the four manufacturing processes employed to produce the product took just six minutes in total.

The product was standing as work in progress between the four processes for over five weeks. So the business was adding value to the product for six minutes and adding cost for almost six weeks. He found that the six weeks was made up of process blocks between several departments.

Order processing, for instance, took three days before the information was passed on to production planning. Production planning took two to three days to plan the order and then the components stood four days between the individual production processes.

He helped the business to remove the process blockages and reduce the lead times to one week. This gave the business competitive advantage.

The MD said, 'We can now deliver just in time rather than just too late…'

Most process improvement lie at the boundary lines both vertical and horizontal. You find them in the white space. The founder of

Microsoft Bill Gates, says, 'A lousy process will consume ten times as many hours as the work itself requires. A good process will eliminate wasted time.'

The quality guru Edwardes Demming said, 'Ninety-six per cent of all problems are not caused by people but occur because of poor systems and processes.'

Eliminating process blocks and disconnects gets rid of boundaries, and when the boundaries disappear most of the politics, 'too busy' excuses and delays disappear as well.

Many of the problems that businesses face internally are created by the lack of co-operation and communication between departments. As one MD said, 'Ninety per cent of our problems would disappear if we talked to each other more internally.'

The 'silo syndrome' is created when departments and teams have more loyalty to their own team than the business overall. They show little interest in or care for departments or teams in other parts of the business.

Sales get an order and 'throw it over the wall' into planning, who 'pass it on' to production, who then give it to dispatch. The lack of communication or business focus between the departments eventually leads to lower levels of customer service externally.

It is reported that customers are five times more likely to leave because of poor business processes than of poor products.

Process blocks and disconnects occur at the intersection between departments or functions. They either don't see each other as internal customers or they do not co-operate very effectively with other teams internally. This creates major blockages and problems.

Story – The American Healthcare System

In the USA the performance of hospitals is published in league tables. Your chance of success from a procedure such as an operation varies quite dramatically between hospitals. For example, it could be 90 per cent in one hospital and 50 per cent in another.

The wide variation in results for the same operations was investigated to try to explain the difference.

Initially, the researchers thought it must be down to better surgeons or more investment or better equipment, but none of these seemed to explain the differences. Eventually the researchers looked at team working between surgeons, nurses, administrators and healthcare workers. Surprisingly, this did correlate and explain the differences.

So removing the process blocks and disconnects and encouraging cross-team working was literally making the difference between life and death.

Here is how to resolve the problem of process blocks and disconnects and improve your processes:

Step 1: Get your people together

Bring your team leaders or department leaders together and tell them you want to improve the service to your customers, reduce internal problems and improve efficiency.

Undertake the ground-rules exercise in the Toolkit 28, 'Fixing system slippage', in order to create the right working environment.

Step 2: Complete Toolkit 8 together

This is the toolkit we call 'Creating a vision for your business'. This will create an overall vision for the business rather than the current focus on departmental goals.

Step 3: Get your people together – again

In order to achieve your business's vision, get your department heads together again and ask each one to state what they want from the internal customers either side of their teams. Ask production planning what they need from sales (upstream from them) and production (downstream). Get them to list their requirements (e.g., eight hours' notice of changes to the production schedule or customer requirements outside the normal spec, confirmed in writing).

Then get them to state what they actually get in practice – for instance, they might need customer requirements to be confirmed in writing but this rarely happens, so mistakes are made and customers complain.

Encourage them to change their practice in line with their internal customer requirements ('You need the planning information by 2 p.m. Wednesday, so we will ensure now that you get it – now we understand why you need it by that time').

Be prepared to find some really stupid disconnects and blockages. In 90 per cent of cases they occur because of poor communication and therefore a lack of understanding and not because people are being deliberately difficult. Sometimes it comes down to a lack of shared standards. For example:

- Sales promise delivery in ten days.
- Production thinks it's fifteen days.
- The MD wants it to be five days.
- Finance don't care: they say, 'We just send out the invoices'.

So agreeing the company's standard for say delivery in ten days is sufficient to clear away many blockages and disconnects.

TIP: If you really want people to co-operate rather than compete ensure the reward system supports the process.

Example

An engineering company on Tyneside reviewed their process blocks and disconnects. The company were promising delivery of components within five days and 100 per cent of deliveries on time to their customers. The sales team were selling service but the bonus scheme for the production department was based on volume.

The production team made what gave them the biggest bonus and consequently ignored the sales team's customer-service promises. The bonus scheme was changed and the customer-service levels improved dramatically.

Step 4: Design a process based on needs

You may find that a process has not been fully developed or people have a different understanding of how it works. They are clear about their bit but not how it works out with the sales team. If this is the case then get your department heads or their nominees to design a process together based on the needs of the business – not their particular interests.

Step 5: Set up team meetings

These should be between the department heads to monitor the 'new internal customer agreements' and deal with problems.

TIP: It is normal for the agenda of meetings to move from problem solving to planning. This is a very positive indicator that the process blocks and disconnects have been removed.

Troubleshooter

Potential problems	Suggested remedies
Identifying blockages between departments gets personal, and people get into 'defensive attacking' mode.	1. Tell them up front this might happen and that you won't stand for it. 2. If a real problem occurs, stop the meeting, take the protagonists to one side and read them the riot act.
Internal team leaders are unable/ unwilling to identify any internal process blocks.	Appoint a small review team to audit the processes and identify the issues.
People perceive the change as discretionary or the internal culture is too ingrained.	1. Conduct an external customer perception survey to provide evidence of the need to change. 2. Calculate the costs and benefits of the improvements to the business of making changes. 3. Consider rewarding people by sharing any improvements with them.
Personality clashes create blockages.	Get them to co-operate or 'change the personalities'. Remember, no individual is more important than your business.

CHAPTER TEN

Cut Costs, Boost Profits

Toolkits 30–31

Toolkit 30: Control your recipe for success
Toolkit 31: Inspect don't expect in order to boost your profits

Toolkit 30: Control your recipe for success

> Develop consistent performance throughout your business.
> ■ Protect your strategy and your competitive edge.
> ■ Sleep easy in your bed (knowing your business is under control).

Successfully implementing plans and strategies consistently over time is a real challenge for many businesses. This toolkit will help you to monitor and manage the critical elements of your business on an ongoing basis by using key indicators.

The critical word is 'key'. Clearly, you need to monitor lots of details in your business. This toolkit helps you to establish and monitor the 7–10 strategic indicators that really matter if your business is to continue to be a success.

Here is an example:

STORY – CompuAdd Computers

> CompuAdd are a computer manufacturer based in Bristol. By monitoring and managing their key indicators they made the following improvements over a six-month period:

	Before		After
Percentage of orders delivered on time	58 per cent	Improved to	96 per cent
Level of quality defects	8 per cent	Reduced to	1 per cent
Level of repeat business	80 per cent	Improved to	92 per cent
Average order size	£10k	Improved to	£15k
Gross margin	30 per cent	Improved to	56 per cent
Level of stock	£500k	Reduced to	£150k
Number of post–sale calls and other measures of customer satisfaction	3	Reduced to	1

Story – Keepmoat PLC

Keepmoat decided that they had two key indicators, which they called drivers. These were cash and return on capital employed.

They established the indicators, communicated them to everyone, developed initiatives to drive them forward and monitored them on a weekly basis.

Over a two-year period, 1998–2000, cash at the bank went from £10 million overdrawn to £10 million positive. Return on capital improved from 18 to 35 per cent.

'The key indicators made us focus on what at that time was important in our business,' said their financial director, David Blunt. 'It reminded us that if you focus on clear objectives and monitor and manage them it is possible to make significant improvements to the business.'

So how do you establish key indicators in your business?

Step 1: Establish strategic indicators

It is helpful to have a broad range of key strategic indicators, not just financial ones. Answer these questions in order to help establish them. At this stage this is a brainstorming exercise, so go for quality as well as quantity.

Q1. What enables us to do business successfully?
E.g., We delight customers so we enjoy high levels of repeat business.

Therefore we need to monitor:
E.g., Levels of customer delight weekly.

Q2. What are our strategic aspirations or priorities?
E.g., To build a valued business.

Therefore we need to monitor:
E.g., Strength of the balance sheet monthly.

> TIP: How are you doing so far? If you find it hard to think of the indicators, remember that it is the acid test of how well you know what really matters in your business. Tough but true, so keep going ...

Q3. What enables us to complete effectively?
E.g., Low-cost production.

Therefore we need to monitor:
E.g., Costs very accurately, monthly.

Q4. What financial targets are critical to meet?
E.g., Net profit –10 per cent.

Therefore we need to monitor:
E.g., Net profit, monthly.

Q5. Where are the bulk of our costs?
E.g., Materials and direct labour make up 90 per cent of all costs.

Therefore we need to monitor:
E.g., Material purchases and utilisation and labour costs and productivity.

Q6. Do we have a key customer service target?
E.g., Delivery within 24 hours.

Therefore we need to monitor:
E.g., Delivery performance daily by making a hundred random calls to customers to ensure we stay above our 98 per cent on-time target.

Q7. Where are we at risk?
E.g., Contracts that are not planned properly in detail, so they end up going wrong and costing us a fortune.

Therefore we need to monitor:
E.g., The use of the precontract planning process on every contract.

Q8. What are the important lessons that we have learned from the past that we need to manage well?

E.g., Don't 'buy' work – i.e., don't tender below cost because we lose money whenever we do too much.

Therefore we need to monitor:

E.g., Gross margin levels at every tender.

Q9. How important is our people's commitment and contribution?

E.g., Critical, we are a people business.

Therefore we need to monitor:

E.g., Our people's attitudes and motivation at least every six months by an independent survey.

Q10. What is critical to our customers that we need to control?

E.g., They say they want to see our directors regularly.

Therefore we need to monitor:

E.g., Effectiveness of director networking plans with key customers.

> TIPS:
> - Get your team to help you to identify your key indicators.
> - Consider a customer perception survey to identify real customer expectations, which you can then monitor.

Step 2: Prioritise the key indicators

You may have identified 20–30 possible indicators in Step 1. By definition they cannot all be key. You can use some of the priority tools (X) to reduce them to 6–8.

1. Consider Toolkit 6 on prioritising and focusing (e.g., 'Our strategy/plan calls for X therefore we need to monitor Y').

2. Search for the domino (see Toolkit 6 'Tools for prioritising and focusing') (e.g., 'Which one will impact most on the rest?')

> TIP: Make sure you choose indicators that monitor customers, operations and employees as well as the financial ones.

3. Get your team to use the priority tools (Toolkit 6 again) and debate and agree the six to eight key indicators.

4. Before you finalise your indicators you might contrast them with some less traditional ones:

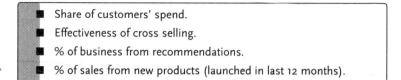

- Share of customers' spend.
- Effectiveness of cross selling.
- % of business from recommendations.
- % of sales from new products (launched in last 12 months).

For example, 3M Innovation has a key strategic indicator: 25 per cent of all sales from products developed within the last four years.

5. Make sure you turn the indicators into measurable statistics – e.g., not 'delighting customers' but 'customers who rate us at 95 per cent plus on our satisfaction survey'.

Do your indicators really monitor your recipe for success? Is there a balance of indicators – e.g., customers, employees, costs, returns etc?

Step 3: monitor and report your key indicators

Set up a system to do this. Put the indicators into your management reporting process. Report on them regularly and frequently to all concerned.

Track the trends in the indicators. Are they going in the right direction?

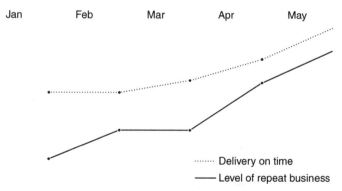

Consider putting trend lines, using linear regression, through the indicators in order to smooth the trends.

This is how some of the best businesses really do control the key aspects of their business. Ask your accountant or IT specialist to help you.

Step 4: Set targets for improvement

Agree with your team, targets for improving the indicators (see CompuAdd and Keepmoat stories).

Be persistent; make the review of the indicators a regular (monthly) ritual in your business with everybody who needs to be involved.

Troubleshooter

Potential problems	Suggested remedies
You measure what's easy (usually financial numbers) rather than what really matters, because they look difficult to measure (e.g. delighting customers).	Don't just let the accountants set up the system. Get your managers involved? Be creative and insistent. For instance, you can measure customer delight by: • levels of repeat business • business from referrals
Indicators not available in standard software package.	Make somebody responsible for recording them properly, possibly using a spreadsheet format.
Some indicators turn out not to be critical over time and others emerge that are critical.	This normally happens. Aim to reduce the indicators over twelve months to six or eight.

Toolkit 31: Inspect, don't expect, in order to boost your profits

 Discover what's really happening in your business.
■ Keep your business standards up to scratch.
■ Stop haemorrhaging profits.

As the CEO or owner of a business, you will appreciate how important it is to keep abreast of the things that are happening day to day in your business. The business grows and then it becomes a more difficult problem to stay in touch due to size and complexity.

Growth demands that the organisation structure be developed and that people be reorganised into departments. It becomes much less easy to keep track of what makes your business really tick and what's happening at the sharp end.

Story – North Staffs Caravans

> Simon Keats, MD of North Staffs Caravans, attended a workshop called 'Inspect, don't expect' and returned to his £4 million caravan retail business to boost his profits.
>
> 'I spent a day in the accounts department working as an accounts clerk alongside the team. I could not believe how generous people were with our money. We were paying invoices without checking and we obviously had some very cosy favourite supplier relationships. I could not believe it. We were throwing cash out of the window. We tightened up and saved over £100k in six months.'

I learned the technique from Sir Anthony Cleaver, who was chairman of six companies in 1996. I asked him how he managed to control six businesses and he told me he focused on three things:

- Setting clear objectives for the business and the top people.
- Ensuring the incentive scheme supports the objective.
- Inspecting, not expecting: go and see for yourself what's really happening in your business at the sharp end.

Step 1: Spend a day with ...

Simon Keats's example of spending a day with his accounts team is one form of inspecting, not expecting.

You could also choose to:

- Spend a day in the field with a salesperson.
- Sit in on a management meeting you don't normally attend.
- Work on the production line for a day.

There are many places to look – but be warned: take Prozac before you do!

But, you may be thinking, Shouldn't I trust my people? Of course you should, but this should not prevent you from inspecting what's really happening once in a while. It's not what you do: it's the way that you do it.

> TIP: Don't confuse delegating and trust with keeping your finger on the pulse. Some managers believe that they should delegate and blindly trust people all the time. This is naïve in my experience.

Step 2: Initiate investigations

While Step 1 is about immersing yourself in parts of your business you don't normally, Step 2 is about personally digging deep into your business to find out what's really going on. Where should you look?

Trust your own intuition. Where do you think that things might not be happening as they should be?

One CEO, for instance, noticed that the number of credit notes being issued was suddenly increasing. He wondered why. On further investigation he found that his business was issuing three times the number of credit notes in 2000 as it did in 1999. This was due to a change of warehouse management and a reduction in the checking of deliveries sent to customers.

Follow the money. Where are your biggest costs? One software company were spending 60 per cent of their costs on subcontractors. Investigating subcontract management revealed some very meaty problems to resolve.

Most businesses have a cost profile of two to three high cost elements: for example, labour and materials account for seventy to eighty per cent of total costs.

Focus on these big cost elements in order to identify opportunities to really boost your profits.

> TIP: Get one of your management accountants to act as your helper for a while. Ask them to dig deep in critical cost areas and find out what's really happening with costs.

Where is your business most at risk? How are your people managing risk? One construction industry CEO inspected the use of his company's risk-management system. They had a policy and a process but it turned out that only 40 per cent of managers actually used them. This put 60 per cent of contracts at legal risk.

Check company supplier relationships. Is anybody benefiting internally from trips to the races or other forms of 'entertainment' without permission?

Check which products or customers make you money. You may be surprised. Very often one or two products or customers produce 80 per cent of the profits. One consultancy business, for instance, found that over ten years every time they worked for a housing association they lost 2 per cent on the contract. Yet when they worked with local authorities they made 2 per cent profit. It was not until this analysis was completed that they changed their customer focus.

Where do you really make and lose money?

The key to this step is to expect nothing. Go looking in any areas you feel may hold the opportunity to cut costs. Change practices. Watch for people spending your money like confetti. As one CEO put it when he found some major cost discrepancies, 'They've had a lot of fun playing at the casino with our chips. That's finished now.'

Step 3: Improve the costing/control systems

Very often one of the conclusions from Steps 1 and 2 in this toolkit is the recognition that the business really does need to upgrade its costing or control systems.

Example

> One housing company's client's financial director was asked to upgrade the costing system. Somehow he never quite got round to it. We didn't smell a rat until we inspected some of the pricing of the executive houses: they were incorrect by a big margin. It transpired that the FD was moving money around on contracts to create a false profit picture. This was not strictly illegal but it did not allow the business to make proper future strategy decisions.
>
> Once an effective costing system was installed we discovered that the company was making a profit on only three home types and losing significant amounts on six others.

A key stake in the ground for all businesses is an effective, accurate and reliable costing system. (I know everybody knows this but you would be amazed how many costing systems are all over the place.)

Step 4: Visit some key customers

Visit some key customers. Take them to lunch and ask them for some honest, direct, straight feedback. How are we really doing? What can we improve? They may tell you things about your business that you had no idea about. That's why you are talking to them.

Step 5: Check your business systems and routines

Sample your systems and routines, particularly those that you don't normally get to see:

- a selection of appraisal reports
- copies of management minutes
- sales reports
- market forecasts
- your sales presentations to key customers
- project reports

You don't need to become a paranoid interfering boss, but you should take the pulse occasionally of what's happening in your business in areas you don't normally get to see. Clearly, while you are inspecting you should be probing.

- 'Give me an example.'
- 'Talk me through that process very slowly step by step...'
- 'Let's get the facts on that one.'
- 'Let's dig deeper here ...'

TIP: Be persistent if you smell a rat. Ask for a detailed report or more information. Don't be fobbed off. My regrets are not about upsetting people but occasionally not digging deeper when my intuition told me something was not quite right.

Troubleshooter

Potential problems	Suggested remedies
Your people accuse you of interfering and not trusting them.	Explain that you are interested in learning about every aspect of the business. Confirm your trust in them.
People 'hide' information or it's not readily available.	Dig deeper. If you meet resistance then you are probably on to something.
Some things need deep analysis, which you don't have the time to undertake.	If it's important enough, then second somebody to do the legwork on your behalf.

CHAPTER ELEVEN

Controlling Your Business

Toolkits 32–33

Toolkit 32: Fighting the flab
Toolkit 33: Keep your finger on the financial pulse of your business

Toolkit 32: Fighting the flab

- Cut out all unnecessary costs.
- Get back to basics – get rid of the flab.
- Raise your own cash internally for investment.

Once businesses move from the entrepreneurial stage, where they watched every penny, into the mature managed stage, they often build in unnecessary costs.

You will be familiar with the annual budgeting and planning cycle: last year's budget with a 10 per cent sales increase and a lot of hope! Fixed costs are normally carried forward year on year and rarely re-examined.

By getting back to basics using a zero-based budgeting process, businesses can free up significant amounts of cash, which can then be reinvested in the areas of the business that create the real profits.

Story – A UK Rail Company

The engineering division of a UK rail company spent £40 million annually on maintaining engines and wagons. A new CEO wanted to cut costs and release cash for investment. He asked the engineering director how much it cost to maintain an engine. He replied, 'We have three hundred locos and spend £15 million annually so divide by three hundred. That's £50k per engine.'

'No,' replied the frustrated CEO, 'you have just taken your costs and divided by the units. I want to know what it actually costs us to maintain an engine, not what your budget has been for the past five years.'

It was found that the actual cost was £35,000 per engine. The rest of his budget was made up of flab and unnecessary overhead costs, which had never been questioned or properly reviewed for a long time.

The purpose of zero-based budgeting is to re-examine the assumptions built into the budgeting or financial planning process in order to cut out unnecessary costs and release cash for investment. You become your own venture capitalist!

Here is the principle of the process; most budgets follow this process.

Sales or cost forecast for the next twelve months (often broken down monthly)

E.g., Months	Dec.	Jan.	Feb.	Mar.	Apr.
Sales '000	100	120	90	180	110
Costs					
Variable					
Wages	20	25	22	26	25
Materials	30	36	25	40	36
Fixed					
Heat	5	5	7	5	6
Light	2	3	2	4	2
Legal fees	0	2	0	4	0
Salaries	20	20	20	20	20
Water	1	2	1	0	0
Profit	5	8	2	10	8

Most budgets follows this process:

1. Sales forecast
2. Costs (based on last year's performance)
3. Profits (what's left when you take sales – costs)

In this approach the sales and costs are relatively fixed and the profit is variable.

Zero-based budgeting changes the assumptions to:

1. Sales estimate (fixed)
2. Profit required (fixed)
3. Costs = variable (i.e., what we can afford)

This process challenges managers to question every cost and also to attempt to make as many fixed costs as possible vary with the sales level: for example, by outsourcing, short-term contracts, sale or return, just-in-time delivery, subcontracting and so on.

Here is how to do it:

Step 1: Establish monthly sales forecast for next 12 months

Step 2: Establish profit requirements

These should be based on your aspirations, not historical results. For instance, the construction industry (contracting) traditionally makes 1–2 per cent net profit. Keepmoat PLC decided they wanted 4 per cent and ended up achieving 3.5 per cent. They broke the traditional mindset of 'We are a 1–2 per-cent-profit industry.'

Step 3: Ask what must be spent

Ask what we *must* spend in order to achieve the sales and profit targets. Cut out all unnecessary costs. Question and challenge every cost.

Look for ways of making fixed costs variable (e.g., make suppliers stockhold). Cut out unproductive overheads such as monthly retainers to PR consultants.

Consider outsourcing or sub-contracting non core activities like cleaning or IT.

Get three quotes for every major cost item, including electricity and water. Renegotiate bank and accountancy charges. Get help from a creative accountant.

Overall, seek to double your traditional profit levels.

> TIP: A health warning: cut out flab and waste, not muscle. In other words, cut things that add cost and not value. Leave the paper clips and the people alone.

Step 4: Monitor your budget

Establish your budget and monitor it carefully every month to ensure no slippages occur, such as variable costs becoming fixed again.

Troubleshooter

Potential problems	Suggested remedies
Some managers want to defend their department costs; it's their empire and they do not want it reducing.	• Give them a share of the savings they make. • Make it mandatory. • Cut your personal overheads to demonstrate commitment to the process.
People have their favourite suppliers.	Make it a company rule, get three quotes for everything. Wal-Mart, for instance, forbid buyers to accept even a sandwich from a supplier. They want low costs, not comfy (costly) relationships.
Some managers 'start counting paper clips' and details, which demotivates people.	Focus on the real cost-reduction opportunities.

Toolkit 33: Keep your finger on the financial pulse of your business

■ Manage your key financial indicators.
■ Control your cash.
■ Manage growth.

This toolkit was jointly developed with Geoff Potts, an expert in 'dynamic accounting' at the Foundation for SME Development at Durham University Business School.

For many businesses, finance and accounting tend to be left to banks and accountants. By leaving your numbers to the 'experts' you may be missing a trick or two. You may be even giving up control of your business.

As the manager of any business, you need to know what makes it profitable (or not) and how to have enough cash available to pay bills at the right time. If your business is growing you want to know how much extra cash you will need and where to get it.

You need to understand the financial consequences of your business decisions on the financial results of your business overall.

Here's how to do it:

Step 1: Manage break-even sales

Break-even sales are simply the sales value you will need in any period to cover all your business costs. Break-even sales analysis helps you to get maximum profits (or minimum losses) by focusing on the three key figures that decide your profit or loss:

- sales
- gross profit as a percentage of sales
- fixed costs (expenses or overheads)

To examine your break-even, you use the following:

Variable costs (nearly always described in your accounts as cost of sales) – these are costs that go up as your sales rise and go down if your sales fall (materials, for example).

Fixed costs (probably described in your accounts as expenses or overheads but other terms are used) – these are costs that stay the same whether your sales go up or down (e.g., rent).

Gross profit – this is the monetary difference between the value of your sales and the cost to you of buying or manufacturing the goods you have sold.

Gross profit percentage (often described as gross margin or gross margin percentage) – this is your gross profit divided by sales multiplied by 100.

Your 'break-even sales point' is the level of sales you need to make for your business to break even (so that it makes neither profit nor loss). It is important to know that your 'break-even sales point' will change over time because of the way it is worked out. You can work out your break-even sales point every day, every week or every month.

Before you can work out your break-even sales you need to work out your gross profit percentage:

Example

Selling price £100,000
Less variable costs £60,000
Gross profit is £ 40,000
Your gross profit percentage is:
Your gross profit divided by your sales and then multiplied by 100.

This is

£ 40,000 × 100

£100,000

giving a gross profit percentage of 40%.

We can now use this information to work out your break-even sales.

Your break-even sales point is:

Your fixed costs divided by your gross profit percentage and then multiplied by 100.

Using the gross profit percentage of 40 per cent, and assuming that your fixed costs are £30,000:

Your break-even sales are:

£30,000 × 100

40%

Plotting break-even sales in relation to sales on a graph is the simplest way of gaining an insight into the profitability of your business. Ideally, break-even sales should be held constant or even be reduced while sales are increasing in a controlled and incremental fashion. In any business where break-even sales are increasing at the same rate or a higher rate than sales, then you may be operating like the proverbial 'busy fool'. This means that you are working increasingly hard to make only the level of profits that were generated at lower levels of turnover, while at the same time the need for cash will be increasing, putting further pressure on the business.

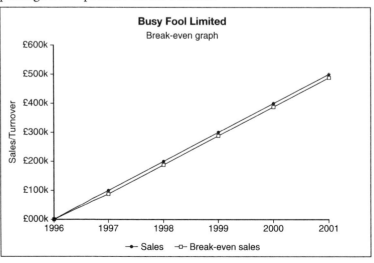

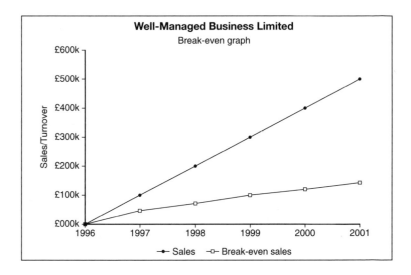

Using break-even to improve your business

If you compare your actual sales with your break-even point, you will be able to see whether you are:

- making a profit (your sales are above your break-even sales point)
- making a loss (your sales are less than your break-even sales point)
- just breaking even (your sales are equal to your break-even sales point)

There are three things you can do to increase profits or reduce losses:

- reduce your break-even sales point while keeping actual sales the same
- increase your sales while keeping your break-even sales point the same
- reduce your break-even sales point and increase your sales at the same time

You can reduce your break-even sales point by:

- improving your gross profit percentage by increasing prices and/or reducing variable costs (cost of sales)

- reducing your fixed costs by cutting your overheads (see Toolkit 32, 'Fighting the flab')
- reviewing your product mix – that is devoting your resources towards selling more of those products or services that produce the highest return (see Toolkit 9 'Redoing your strategy in order to revitalise your business')

Improving gross profit %

All businesses should try to improve their gross profit percentage through modest price increases and reductions in the cost of sales. Unfortunately, the most frequent reaction during times of difficulty is to reduce prices with a view to generating additional sales income. This ignores the simple fact that the whole of any price reduction must come out of the profit. This is best illustrated by reference to the Price/Volume Dynamic Ready Reckoner below.

Cutting prices

Percentage that sales must increase to maintain current gross profit

Current gross profit percentage

Price cut %	10%	20%	25%	30%	35%	40%	45%	50%
−2%		25%	11%	9%	7%	6%	5%	5%	4%
−3%		43%	18%	14%	11%	9%	8%	7%	6%
−4%		67%	25%	19%	15%	13%	11%	10%	9%
−5%		100%	33%	25%	20%	17%	14%	13%	11%
−10%			100%	67%	50%	40%	33%	29%	25%
−15%			300%	150%	100%	75%	60%	50%	43%

Example

A business achieving a 40 per cent gross profit that cuts prices by 10 per cent will need to generate 33 per cent additional sales before starting to improve on the pre-price-cut trading position. This could be catastrophic, as the hardest thing to generate during a recession or times of adversity is additional sales. Then you have to consider whether the additional level of activity required is feasible with existing physical resources and whether you have enough cash available to cover the additional working capital required.

Increasing prices
Percentage that sales can fall before total gross profit reduces

Current gross profit percentage

Price increase	10%	20%	25%	30%	35%	40%	45%	50%
+2%	17%	9%	7%	6%	5%	5%	4%	4%
+3%	23%	13%	11%	9%	8%	7%	6%	6%
+4%	29%	17%	14%	12%	10%	9%	8%	7%
+5%	33%	20%	17%	14%	13%	11%	10%	9%
+10%	50%	33%	29%	25%	22%	20%	18%	17%
+15%	60%	43%	37%	33%	30%	27%	25%	23%

Example

> If a business with a 40 per cent gross profit margin increases prices by 10 per cent, it can afford to lose 20 per cent of volume without suffering any reduction in profit levels. If sales fall by less than 10 per cent, then the business is generating more profit, without anyone having to work any harder. At the same time the reduction in sales will take the pressure off resources and free up cash previously tied up in working capital.

> TIP: Know why your customers buy from you rather than your competitors – it is unlikely to be price alone. Conduct a customer perception survey to identify why your customers buy from you (see Toolkit 16, 'Conducting a customer perception survey').

Calculations based on our earlier example:

Sales	£100,000
Variable costs	£60,000
Gross profit	£40,000 (40%)
Fixed costs	£30,000
Net profit	£10,000 (10%)
Break-even sales	£75,000

The effect of increasing price

If you increase the selling price by 10 per cent, sales income will increase from £100,000 to £110,000 while variable and fixed costs remain the same. Accordingly, gross profit will increase by £10,000 from £40,000 to £50,000, gross profit percentage will increase from 40 per cent to 45.5 per cent, break-even sales will fall from £75,000 to £65,934 and net profit will double from £10,000 to £20,000.

This is illustrated below:

Sales	£100,000	£110,000
Variable costs	£ 60,000	£ 60,000
Gross profit	£ 40,000 (40%)	£ 50,000 (45.5%)
Fixed costs	£ 30,000	£ 30,000
Net profit	£ 10,000 (10%)	£ 20,000 (18.2%)
Break-even sales	£ 75,000	£ 65,934

If prices are increased by 10 per cent and sales remain constant, then net profit will increase by 100 per cent and break-even sales will fall by 12 per cent.

> TIP: Avoid trying to stimulate turnover by cutting prices, since you will almost certainly find yourself suffering from the 'busy fool' syndrome.

Reducing variable costs (cost of sales)

So far we have looked only at the effect of a change in price. Another possibility is to reduce variable costs, which is also known as 'value engineering'. Most businesses can reorganise their operational processes to reduce the labour and material content of production. See, for example, Toolkit 28, 'Fixing system slippage', and Toolkit 29, 'Removing process blocks and disconnects'. Cumulatively, small changes and marginal trimming can be extremely significant and bring about noticeable results. The combined effect of cost reductions and effective pricing can substantially improve the financial performance of any business.

Using our example again, if you reduce variable costs by 10 per cent, they will fall from £60,000 to £54,000. Accordingly, gross profit will increase by £6,000 from £40,000 to £46,000, gross profit percentage will increase from 40 per cent to 46 per cent, break-even sales will fall from £75,000 to £65,217 and net profit will increase £6,000 to £16,000.

This is illustrated below:

Sales	£100,000	£100,000
Variable costs	£ 60,000	£ 54,000
Gross profit	£ 40,000 (40%)	£ 46,000 (46%)
Fixed costs	£ 30,000	£ 30,000
Net profit	£ 10,000 (10%)	£ 16,000 (16%)
Break-even sales	£ 75,000	£ 65,217

If variable costs are reduced by 10 per cent, net profit will increase by 62.5 per cent and break-even sales will fall by 13 per cent.

Step 2: Controlling gross profit

Gross profit is the difference between the value of sales for a specific period and the variable costs the business incurs because of those sales. These costs will be described in your accounts as cost of sales.

This difference or gross profit is what your business has generated in order to pay for the fixed costs of the business, such as rent, rates, your salary, salaries of managers, telephones and stationery. Anything left over is net profit for the business.

Once you have met your variable costs:

- If your gross profit is not enough to pay for all the fixed costs of your business then you have made a loss.
- If your gross profit is just enough to pay for your fixed costs then you have broken even.
- If your gross profit is more than enough to pay your fixed costs then you have made a profit.
- If you are in control of your gross profit then you are in control of one of the key factors that directly affect how profitable your business is. (The others are sales and fixed costs.)

Your aim is very simple – you must get your gross profit in pounds as high as possible for your product or service. If you can do this, you are more likely to be able to pay all your fixed costs and earn a net profit as well.

Step 3: Control fixed costs

Fixed costs are those costs that your business will continue to incur for some time, even if you stopped making or selling your products or services today. These include rent on your premises, business rates, insurance and many others. Do not forget to include any interest paid here.

There are lots of views on what is and what is not a fixed cost, which makes it very confusing for everyone, even the accountant. The best way of dealing with this particular problem is simply to be consistent in how you split your costs because you will then be able to compare key trends accurately within your business.

> TIP: When looking to cut fixed costs, focus on 'good housekeeping' but be careful not to damage your business fundamentally. It will still be necessary to invest in the research and development of new products, new processes, new markets, the introduction of new technology and in your staff if the business is to prosper in the long term.

If you reduce fixed costs by 10 per cent they will fall by £3,000 from £30,000 to £27,000. Accordingly, the gross profit and gross profit percentage will remain unchanged, but break-even sales will fall from £75,000 to £67,500 and net profit will increase £6,000 to £16,000.

This is illustrated below:

Sales	£100,000	£100,000
Variable costs	£ 60,000	£ 60,000
Gross profit	£ 40,000 (40%)	£ 40,000 (40%)
Fixed costs	£ 30,000	£ 27,000
Net profit	£ 10,000 (10%)	£ 16,000 (16%)
Break-even sales	£ 75,000	£ 67,500

If variable costs are reduced by 10 per cent net profit will increase by 30 per cent and break-even sales will fall by 10 per cent.

> TIP: Consider completing the 'Fighting the flab' toolkit 32 in order to attack and reduce your fixed costs.

> TIP: Try to make as many fixed costs as variable as possible (for instance, pay your PR company for projects, not a retainer).

To improve profitability and reduce break-even, increasing prices and reducing variable and fixed costs is a winning combination. Let us see the cumulative effect of a 10 per cent increase in price and a 10 per cent reduction in both variable costs and fixed costs.

This is illustrated below:

Sales	£100,000	£110,000
Variable costs	£ 60,000	£ 54,000
Gross profit	£ 40,000 (40%)	£ 56,000 (50.9%)
Fixed costs	£ 30,000	£ 27,000
Net profit	£ 10,000 (10%)	£ 29,000 (26.4%)
Break-even sales	£ 75,000	£ 53,045

The combined result of these changes is that net profit has increased by £19,000 to £29,000 (up 190 per cent) while break-even sales have fallen by £21,955 (down 29 per cent).

Key points

All businesses should focus on improving their gross profit.

Gross profit is the small number that is the difference between two large numbers, sales and variable costs (costs of sales). Small changes in the large numbers will lead to large changes in the small number.

The combined effect of 'value engineering' (reducing cost of sales) and modest increases in price will substantially improve the profitability of any business.

The whole effect of any reduction in price can only come out of the gross profit. The sensitivity of the price–volume relationship must always be a prime consideration.

A growing business is only 'better off' by the additional profit or contribution, not additional turnover.

Step 4: Control cash

To stay in business today and in the future, your business must be generating enough cash to pay the bills at the time when they have to be paid. Unless you have enough cash available, it does not matter how 'profitable' your business is, because the people to whom you owe money (your creditors) will not wait to be paid.

For a small business, it is shortage of ready cash to pay the bills today that leads to failure, even if the business is profitable. Cash is the short-term necessity while profit is needed in the medium to long term. It is important to focus on cash first, then profits and finally growth. In practice, too many owners of small businesses get this 100 per cent the wrong way around. They focus on growth, then profits and finally cash, only to discover it is too late to save their business in the cash crisis that follows.

When thinking of the flow of cash into and out of your business, there are three things you can control:

- debtors – customers who owe you money
- stock – materials, products in the process of being made and finished goods
- creditors – suppliers and others you owe money to

Think of debtors as the main flow of cash into your business and creditors as the main flow out. Stock represents the stage in between and needs to be kept to a minimum, although you need to have your products available when customers want them. They are a temporary store of your cash, which you need to convert into sales as quickly as possible. There are other flows in and out, but these are the three you must control and use to your advantage. Together they form the working capital of your business.

Day to day, some of the 'cash' available to your business is spread out among creditors, stock and debtors, so you cannot use it to pay bills. Together with any cash you have in the 'till' or at the bank, this is your working capital, which flows around the working-capital cycle below:

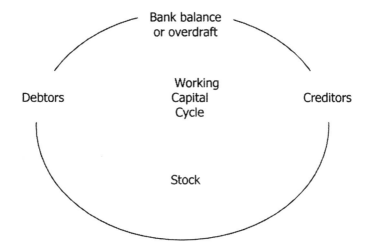

Your aim is to make sure that the right amount of cash is in the right place at the right time.

Debtors

There are a number of steps you should take in order to tighten up your debtor control and ease your cash situation.

- Take up credit references on all new customers. Credit agencies can supply summary details of their accounts and you can also approach their suppliers and bankers for their opinion.
- Make sure that customers know your standard terms and conditions of payment in writing. Confirm them again by sending an acknowledgment of their order and enclosing your terms and

conditions of payment. This way they take precedence over your customers' terms and conditions.

- Make sure your invoices are accurate in every detail – errors give your customers excuses for delay. Invoices should be addressed to the correct person – ring and find out who that is if necessary.

- Send out invoices as early as you can and wherever possible to arrive before the last day of the month end (so they can be processed straightaway).

- Keep an up-to-date list of the credit that has been given to each customer using an aged-debtor list. Make sure someone is responsible for ringing customers as soon as a payment is overdue. Once a regular customer knows you are monitoring late payment and that they can expect a telephone call, they will make sure you are paid on time. After all, who wants to have to 'fob off' suppliers with lame excuses?

- If a customer says 'the cheque is in the post' or gives a date that they will pay by, you must follow this up if you do not receive payment. Nobody likes to be exposed for breaking their promises.

For customers who persistently pay late, you have to decide how much this is costing you and how important the customer is. No customer is worth it if they are going to put you out of business. You can:

- insist on cash payment before delivery
- give a small percentage discount for paying early (you can build this into your margin) or add a credit charge
- increase your price to meet the extra cost of late payment
- decide not to do business
- keep the right to withdraw the goods in your contract if you can

For larger debts that are long overdue or in dispute, take legal advice. An initial consultation to see what chance of success you have may be free, or there may be a fixed fee. If overdue debt is a persistent problem for your business, you could:

- employ a credit agency to chase payment on your behalf
- use an agency that 'factors' your debt, giving you immediate payment of part of every invoice (your banker or local chamber of trade should be able to put you in touch with factoring agencies)

You may be able to take out insurance against bad debts if it would seriously affect your survival.

Getting control of the amount your customers owe you takes time and effort, which you could spend getting more business. But unless you have control of your debtors you might find you have no business at all.

Stock control

The key to good stock control is to break down the totals for raw materials, work in progress and finished goods into individual product lines. Look at each one in turn and relate the stock value to how often it is used (raw materials) or to sales (finished goods). You can then identify:

- Redundant products, which are not used or not being sold. You need to get rid of these in whatever way you can. Tell your accountant so that he or she can consider writing these off in your accounts.
- Slow-moving products, which are not used or sold often. Try a special clearance offer to boost sales and reduce stocks to a more realistic level.
- Fast-moving products, which are used or sold quickly. Make sure you have enough stock to keep production going and to meet orders.

If your work in progress (WIP) is too high, you need to look at what is holding up your production process. Until you have turned raw materials into finished goods, you cannot sell or invoice for them, so your priority is to get them through your process and sold to customers.

In service and contracting businesses, your aim is to get your work to an agreed point at which you can invoice.

Creditors

Suppliers keep your business going by providing the goods (such as raw materials) and services (such as delivery service) that you need to do business with your customers. If your suppliers stop supplying you because you are not paying them on time, and no one else will supply you because you have poor credit references, then your business will grind to a halt. Creditors can even force your business to close if you do not pay what is due, which means you need to be in control of your payments to creditors so that they continue to supply you.

Many businesses take the simplistic view that they should delay payment to creditors for as long as possible to get maximum benefit for themselves. This is especially true for large businesses, which have greater 'clout' with suppliers, especially if the supplier is a small business.

There is an alternative approach to doing business: you can treat suppliers as 'partners' who should not be squeezed as hard as you can get away with. For a small business, this approach is more likely to benefit you and your suppliers in the long run. For instance, suppliers will feel more inclined to help you out if your business has a problem with supply because they like doing business with you. Also, they are more likely to accept an occasional late payment if they know you have a short-term problem.

If you keep to the terms of payment, you maintain a good relationship, which can be of great benefit when you really need the supplier's help.

Keepmoat PLC operate under the Egan principles of supply-chain management. This means they have agreements with key preferred suppliers, which include paying them promptly. Some of the suppliers are taking this partnership approach really to heart and providing business opportunities for Keepmoat with their customers. This is true partnership in practice.

Step 5 Manage growth

Growth can refer to many different things: sales, product range, market share, size, number of employees, outlets and so on. Growth in all of these things can be good for the ego, but it may mean working harder for the same or less return.

Successful businesses focus on growth in profit. To make your business more profitable you do not have to grow in terms of sales, size, product range or any of the things listed above. In fact many businesses have improved profits by:

- getting rid of unprofitable turnover (the big customer, who squeezes your margin, demands extra service and pays very late)
- dropping products that lose money
- reducing size through cutting overheads, number of outlets and so on

Before considering growth, go back to your break-even sales analysis and focus on what you can do: reduce your fixed costs and improve your gross profit percentage.

You can improve your gross profit by getting better prices – increasing prices and dropping unprofitable customers and products – or reducing material and employee costs.

Having set up a sound base for growth by controlling your gross profit and fixed costs, you should then consider the consequences of growth. The real danger with growth is that it can happen too quickly and in an uncontrolled way. If a business grows like this, a number of things happen:

- the owner-manager loses control of events through the sheer complexity and speed of change
- the owner-manager loses touch with customers and the people in the business
- the business adds costs at least as quickly as it adds income – and so it becomes less profitable for more effort

A huge amount of cash can be needed to fund growth. A manufacturing business will typically need £200–300 extra working capital for every additional £1,000 of sales. A service business, which carries little stock, will typically need £120–150 extra working capital for every additional £1,000 of sales. And a retail business, which will have few debtors if any, will typically need £80–120 extra working capital for every additional £1,000 of sales. If this extra cash is not available you end up with a cash-flow crisis and even liquidation.

There have been many studies about the way successful small businesses grow. The main conclusion is that controlled step-by-step growth, with careful short-term and long-term planning, is the best way because:

- it allows owner-managers to stay in control of events and in touch with customers and people as they change to a 'team-managed' business
- you keep control of your break-even sales point and can make the most profit
- you can predict how much cash you will need and arrange the funding in advance

By looking at each of these in turn you can expand your business successfully.

How to stay in touch with customers and people

This is one of the big problems in a growing business, but, as long as you realise this, you are at least halfway to solving the problem.

As your business grows you will need to bring in other people to manage parts of it. Managing your business through others means you will have to learn new skills so you can delegate effectively, confident that you remain in touch and in control. (See Toolkit 15 'Let go to grow'.)

How to get maximum profits

By knowing your break-even sales point month by month and projecting it into the future, you will be able to control how profitable you are (see Step 1).

Make sure your actual sales grow more quickly than your break-even sales point. Many businesses that are growing find they add costs and reduce margins, which means the break-even sales point rises more quickly than sales.

How to predict funding needs

Growing faster than your funds allow you to is guaranteed to give you sleepless nights. You must control your use of cash and predict and arrange funding for growth

You can predict the funding you will need for growth by working out the difference between what you need next year and what you will have available. The difference is your estimated funding requirement.

You can also use specially developed computer software to try different 'what if?' options (such as 'What if gross margin percentage is lower than I thought?' or 'What if more working capital is needed?'

For smaller businesses that may not have accountants in house, simple worksheets enable you to keep your finger on the financial pulse of your business.

Doing the business

I wish you the very best of luck in using the toolkits to boost your company's fortunes. I would be very happy to help you use the toolkits effectively. Email me if you need any help or support on david@davidhalluk.com.

Visit my website www.davidhalluk.com for more information about my work.

Bibliography

Barrow, Paul, *The Bottom Line*, Virgin Publishing, 2001.

Chase, RB, and Daso, S, 'Want to Perfect Your Company's Service Use Behavioural Science', *Harvard Business Review*, June 2001.

Craven, Robert, *Kick-Start Your Business*, Virgin Publishing, 2001

De Gaus, A, *The Living Company*, Nicholas Brealey Publishing, 1999.

Egan, G, *Adding Value*, Jossey-Bass, 1993.

Hall, D, *The Hallmarks for Successful Business*, Management Book 2000 Ltd, 1992.

Hall, D, *In the Company of Heroes*, Kogan Page, 1999.

Kennedy, G, *Everything is Negotiable*, Arrow Books Limited, 1993.

Kline, N, *Time to Think*, Ward Lock, 1999.

Kotter, JP, and Heskett, JL, *Corporate Culture and Performance*, The Free Press, 1992.

O'Shea, J, and Madigan, C, *Dangerous Company*, Nicholas Brealey Publishing, 1997.

Robbins, H, and Finly, M, *Why Teams Don't Work*, Orion Publishing Group Limited, 1997.

Woodroffe, S, *The Book of Yo*, Capstone Publishing Ltd, 2000.

Index

CENTRE FOR SMALL & MEDIUM SIZED ENTERPRISES

Warwick is one of a handful of European business schools that have won a truly global reputation. Its high standards of both teaching and research are regularly confirmed by independent ratings and assessments.

The Centre for Small & Medium Sized Enterprises (CSME) is one of the school's major research centres. We have been working with people starting a business, or already running one, since 1985. The Centre also helps established companies to reignite the entrepreneurial flame that is essential for any modern business.

We don't tell entrepreneurs what to do – just help them be more aware and better informed of the opportunities and pitfalls of running a growing small enterprise.

Much of our practical knowledge is gleaned from the experience of individuals who themselves have been there and done it. These kinds of business coaches rarely commit their observations to paper, but in this Virgin/Warwick series they have captured in print their passion and their knowledge. It's a new kind of business publishing that addresses the constantly evolving challenge of business today.

For more information about Warwick Business School (courses, owner networks and other support to entrepreneurs, managers and new enterprises), please contact:

Centre for Small & Medium Sized Enterprises
Warwick Business School
University of Warwick
Coventry CV4 7AL
UK
Tel: +44 (0) 2476 523741 (CSME); or 524306 (WBS)
Fax: +44 (0) 2476 523747 (CSME); or 523719 (WBS)
Email: enquiries@wbs.warwick.ac.uk
And visit the Virgin/CSME pages via:
www.wbs.warwick.ac.uk